Investigating accs

A workbook for employers, unions, safety representatives
and safety professionals

HSE
BOOKS

ORDER FORM

Ordered by

Title	Initial	Surname
Job title		Company name
Delivery address		
Postcode		Telephone

Email Alert Service

We offer an information service via email. If you would like to be kept informed in this way simply provide your email address

My email address is:

Please send me

ISBN	Title/description	Unit price	Quantity	Total price
0 7176 2827 2	Investigating accidents and incidents	£9.50		£
				£

Total   £

Payment Details

I enclose a cheque/PO* for £ _____ made payable to 'HSE Books'

or Please debit my Mastercard/Visa/American Express* with the amount of £

Card no. [ ][ ][ ][ ] [ ][ ][ ][ ] [ ][ ][ ][ ] [ ][ ][ ][ ]   Start date [ ][ ][ ][ ]   Expiry date [ ][ ][ ][ ]

Cardholder's name   Signature

or Please charge my HSE Books Account No. [ ][ ][ ][ ] [ ][ ][ ][ ] [ ][ ][ ][ ] [ ][ ][ ][ ]

My reference   *Delete as appropriate

The information you provide may be used by us for direct marketing purposes to inform you of new and revised publications.

*If you do **not** wish your name to be used for this purpose, please tick here* [ ]

Return this form to: HSE Books, PO Box 1999, Sudbury, Suffolk CO10 2WA
                    Tel: 01787 881165 Fax: 01787 313995 www.hsebooks.co.uk

HSE priced products are also available through good booksellers

HSE website: www.hse.gov.uk   06/04   161

Out of **CONTROL**

Why control systems go wrong and how to prevent failure

HSE BOOKS

CONTENTS

PREFACE TO 2ND EDITION *iv*

SUMMARY *v*

INTRODUCTION *1*

SECTION ONE: THE LEGAL FRAMEWORK *5*

SECTION TWO: CONTROL SYSTEMS AS SAFETY-RELATED SYSTEMS *7*

SECTION THREE: CONTROL SYSTEM FAILURES *13*

SECTION FOUR: ANALYSIS OF INCIDENTS *44*

SECTION FIVE: MANAGERIAL RESPONSIBILITIES *47*

SECTION SIX: CONCLUSIONS *49*

APPENDIX ONE: SUMMARY OF CAUSES *54*

APPENDIX TWO: SAFETY LIFECYCLE MODEL *56*

APPENDIX THREE: THE LEGAL FRAMEWORK *68*

REFERENCES *75*

GLOSSARY *80*

PREFACE TO 2ND EDITION

The analysis of control system incidents in this publication remains unchanged from the first edition published in 1995. Although there have been substantial advances in control system technology since then, both the overall findings and the more detailed lessons remain applicable and valid today.

For this reprint there has been a comprehensive revision of references. Also some minor changes in the guidance have been made in response to revisions of legislation and of relevant standards.

SUMMARY

The main purpose of this publication is to raise awareness of the technical causes of control system failure by publicising the details of incidents that have been reported or pointed out to the Health and Safety Executive (HSE). Consequently, the contents will be of most interest to managers, engineers, and technicians who hold responsibility at appropriate phases in the lifecycle of a control system.

The analysis of the incidents shows that the majority were not caused by some subtle failure mode of the control system, but by defects that could have been anticipated if a systematic risk-based approach had been used throughout the life of the system. It is also clear that despite differences in the underlying technology of control systems, the safety principles needed to prevent failure remain the same.

Specification

The analysis shows that a significant percentage of incidents can be attributed to inadequacies in the specification of the control system. This may have been due either to poor hazard analysis of the equipment under control (EUC), or to inadequate assessment of the impact of failure modes of the control system on the specification. Whatever the cause, situations that should have been identified are often missed because a systematic approach has not been used. It is difficult to incorporate the changes required to deal with the late identification of hazards after the design process has begun, and more difficult (and expensive) to make such changes later in the life of the control system. It is preferable to expend resources eliminating a problem, rather than to expend resources in dealing with its effects.

Design

Close attention to detail is essential in the design of all safety-related control systems, whether they are simple hard-wired systems, or complex systems implemented by software. It is important that safety analysis techniques are used to ensure that the requirements in the specification are met, and that the foreseeable failure modes of the control system do not compromise that specification. Issues of concern that have been identified include an over-optimistic dependence on the safety integrity of single channel systems, failure to adequately verify software, and poor consideration of human factors. Good design can also eliminate, or at least reduce, the chance of error on the part of the operator or maintenance technician.

Maintenance and modification

The safety integrity of a well-designed system can be severely impaired by inadequate operational procedures for carrying out the maintenance and modification of safety-related systems. Training of staff, inadequate safety analysis, inadequate testing and inadequate management control of procedures are recurring themes of operational failures. This publication gives:

- guidance on the legal requirements relating to control systems;
- information about a systematic, risk-based approach to the design, engineering, operation, maintenance and modification of control systems - the safety lifecycle;
- an analysis of incidents with causes and solutions; and
- references to HSE publications and other sources of advice on preventing control system failure.

INTRODUCTION

1 This publication is aimed firstly at those concerned with the technical aspects of the specification, design, fabrication, commissioning, and maintenance of control systems. The book may also help those responsible for purchasing such systems, or reviewing the safety of existing equipment.

2 However, in the achievement of safety, human and management factors are also very important[1, 2, 3]. Therefore this guidance not only applies to technical managers in the control and instrumentation field, but also to those at senior level in companies that supply and purchase control equipment. These managers carry the responsibility for ensuring that the equipment is competitively priced, and that its safety integrity is adequate in operation. The systematic approach advocated in this document will help to ensure that optimum solutions will emerge in terms of cost and safety. A general study[4] made by HSE into the cost of accidents showed that the costs of error rectification far exceeded those that would have been incurred if a systematic approach had been employed from the outset (see Figure 1 for examples of hidden costs).

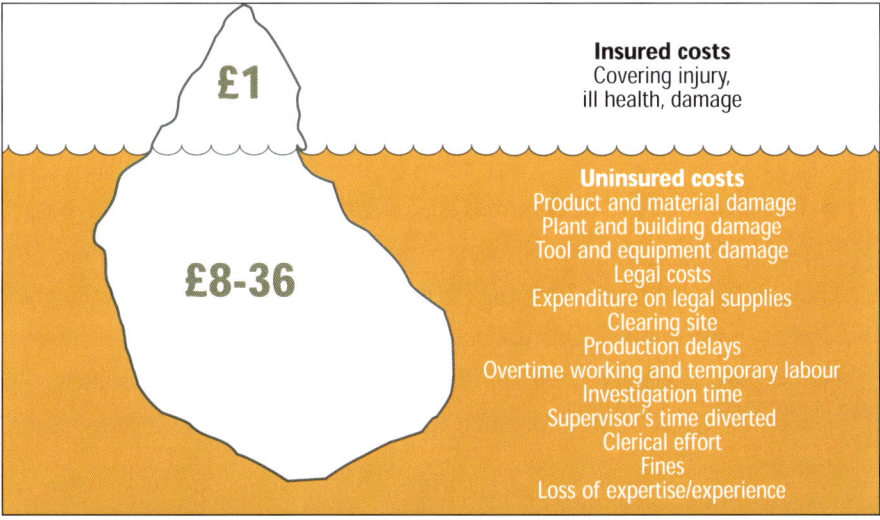

Insured costs
Covering injury,
ill health, damage

£1

Uninsured costs
Product and material damage
Plant and building damage
Tool and equipment damage
Legal costs
Expenditure on legal supplies
Clearing site
Production delays
Overtime working and temporary labour
Investigation time
Supervisor's time diverted
Clerical effort
Fines
Loss of expertise/experience

£8-36

Figure 1: Accident iceberg - the hidden cost of accidents

3 Control systems are an important and pervasive part of modern industry. They range from simple devices, eg a temperature sensor operating a switch that controls a heating element, to complex computer-controlled systems with many inputs and outputs. Control systems may also include the human operator and associated human factor issues surrounding the design of the operator/machine interface. Control systems can be based upon many technologies including hydraulic, pneumatic, electric, electronic, programmable electronic and mechanical.

4 Increased automation has the potential to lead to safer working environments in many traditionally dangerous industries. This is because effective implementation requires minute attention to every detail of the processes involved, resulting in greater awareness of potential hazards. However, failures in control systems have been implicated in accidents and dangerous occurrences. Consequently, this publication is meant to raise awareness of the causes of control system failure by:

- publicising the details of selected examples of such incidents involving control systems; and
- showing how they could have been prevented by the application of straightforward precautions. The details of the incidents were either advised to HSE, or taken from its own internal investigation reports.

5 As this publication was being produced, a number of significant developments involving control systems took place. Firstly a number of regulations and European Directives came into force that specifically addressed control systems. Secondly, work in developing standards for control systems, both at European and international levels, was coming to fruition. It was therefore decided to broaden the scope of the publication to include guidance on these latter developments.

6   Section one provides a brief overview of the legislation applicable to safety-related control systems, and highlights the main requirements of the Regulations. See Appendix three for more detailed information. Of particular importance are the regulations associated with management's responsibilities to carry out an assessment of the risks involved, and to ensure that a systematic approach is used for the effective planning, organisation, control, monitoring and review of safety systems.

7   Section two discusses briefly how control systems can be used as safety-related systems, and introduces the concept of the 'safety lifecycle' as a method of structuring the work required to achieve the necessary level of safety for the machine or process. In particular, the importance of hazard identification is stressed, because it is safer to 'design hazards out', and less expensive overall, than to 'add on' control or protective systems.

8   Section three adopts the safety lifecycle introduced in Section two and for each phase, eg specification, describes a number of incidents where failure of the control system can be traced back to errors and mistakes made in that phase. In discussing the incidents, their causes and solutions, it is important to note that only the most significant points are given. **In particular, the actions taken to overcome the incidents are only given in general technical terms and do not include the full engineering specification and safety management actions needed to properly produce a solution.**

9   Section four gives an overall summary of the 34 incidents analysed for this document.

10 Section five highlights the importance of managerial responsibilities, since it is acknowledged that failures in control systems are not due to technical aspects alone; human and managerial factors are extremely important. Issues such as

conflicting managerial priorities and incentives, lack of safety engineering training, absence of a 'safety culture' and poor contract procedures etc may contribute significantly to an eventual failure that has a technical cause.

11 Section six lists the conclusions that HSE believes can be drawn from the analysis. Appendix one contains a complete list of the incidents that were analysed for this publication, and an overview of the safety lifecycle model is included in Appendix two. Additional information on legislation as it affects control systems is included in Appendix three.

12 Also included at the back of this publication are references and a glossary of terms used in the text that may be unfamiliar to some readers.

SECTION ONE: THE LEGAL FRAMEWORK

Health and Safety at Work etc Act 1974

13 This Act places duties on employers and others to secure the health, safety and welfare of persons at work, and to protect the public from risks arising from work activities. Specific responsibilities are placed on employers, the self-employed, and employees. The Act also places duties on designers, manufacturers, importers and suppliers to ensure that equipment for use at work is designed and manufactured so as to be, so far as is reasonably practicable, safe and without risk to health when used, cleaned, and maintained etc.

14 The duties laid down by this Act have been amplified by more specific legislation, often in the form of regulations made under the Act: some of these have also served to replace much of the pre-1974 legislation. The impetus behind some new health and safety legislation has been provided by the need to implement European Community Directives.

The European Dimension

15 The European Commission (EC) has introduced a number of Directives on health and safety matters. Some of these lay down minimum requirements, which are intended to form the basis of harmonised workplace health and safety laws throughout the Member States of the EC. New regulations have been introduced in the UK to implement these Directives, including:

- The Management of Health and Safety at Work Regulations 1999;
- The Provision and use of Work Equipment Regulations 1998; and
- The Health and Safety (Display Screen Equipment) Regulations 1992.

16 Other EC Directives, sometimes known as New Approach Directives, aim to remove barriers to trade that may arise from different design and

manufacturing standards among Member States. The most significant of these is the Machinery Directive, which the Department of Trade and Industry has implemented in the UK as the Supply of Machinery (Safety) Regulations 1992 (as amended in 1994).

17 A summary of the main requirements of the above regulations that affect control systems is given in Appendix three.

SECTION TWO: CONTROL SYSTEMS AS SAFETY-RELATED SYSTEMS

18 Although there are wider definitions of this term, we define a control system as a system that responds to input signals from the plant and/or an operator and causes the plant or equipment to operate in the desired manner. The plant or equipment that is being controlled is designated as the equipment under control (EUC) - see Figure 2.

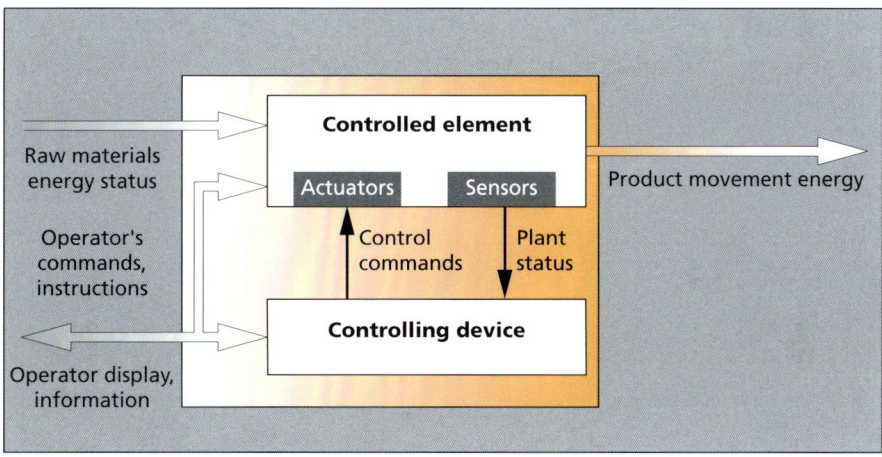

Figure 2: Equipment under control

19 If the control system has a safety role, either as an integral part of the EUC or as a separate protection system, it will be a safety-related system. However it should be noted that it is rare for the whole of safety to be assigned to a control or protection system - other safety-related systems are usually required, eg pressure relief valves and operator procedures.

20 Control systems usually involve one or more input devices, a controller, one or more output devices, power supplies, and any associated information connections. They may not require frequent interaction with operators, but

where these interactions do occur, considerations must be given to human factors[5, 6, 7, 8, 9], eg the way in which information is presented to the operator on a VDU screen.

21 Input devices may be two state, ie either 'on' or 'off', such as pressure or temperature switches, or may be analogue, where continuous signals are sent that correspond to the value of the parameter being sensed. In the latter case, the measured value may be converted into a digital signal by the device before transmission. 'Smart' devices have built-in electronic circuits for this purpose and can perform additional functions.

22 Output devices include such items as motorised or solenoid-operated valves, contactors which switch motors on and off, electrically-operated clutches and brakes, or a complete electronic sub-assembly, eg a variable-speed motor control system.

23 The control system may be implemented by electric, electronic, pneumatic, or hydraulic devices, and may vary in complexity from a simple switch to a programmable electronic device or system.

24 Designing control systems to make plant and equipment functionally safe is a large subject and therefore only a brief overview can be given here. Further advice can be found in IEC 61508[10] and other standards[11, 12], HSE and professional guidance material[13, 14, 15], other publications[16, 17] and in the discussion of incidents in Section three.

25 The application of the safety lifecycle model described at Appendix two is one way of systematically identifying what safety role the control system should perform, and of minimising design and implementation errors. This involves:

- hazard and risk analysis;

- a systematic approach to design, engineering, operation, maintenance and modification; and

- a knowledge of the strengths and weaknesses of control systems as implemented in the various technologies.

26 Typical examples of control systems used to make plant and equipment safe are 'interlocking' and 'protection' systems, but in certain cases these may need to be combined with the process or machine control systems.

Interlocking

27 Interlocking is a means of preventing access to a place containing a hazardous part or process, while allowing access when the hazard is not present. The interlock may be a totally mechanical system or an integral part of the control system, and is often implemented using simple robust components, eg safety limit switches and relays. Further information can be found in relevant British and European standards[12, 18, 19].

Protection systems

28 A protection system is a particular form of control system, often incorporating the continuous monitoring of plant state. It may be a single mechanical device, such as a safety valve, or a separate instrument system, eg the emergency shutdown system of a large petrochemical installation.

29 Protection systems are 'operate on demand' systems, and their main purpose is to bring plant or equipment to a safe state when an operating parameter exceeds safety limits. It is important for protection systems to be frequently proof-tested to ensure that they are available to carry out their

Figure 3: Example of computer-controlled machinery with interlocked access

safety role. Programmable techniques allow automatic self-testing to be applied more widely than is possible with purely electromechanical systems. Sensors, actuators, controllers and interconnecting cabling can all be continually monitored during the operation of the machine or process. Automatic self-testing is increasingly being employed in systems requiring a high safety integrity.

30 Further information can be found in IEC 61508[10], HSE and professional guidance material[13, 14, 15], other publications[16, 17, 20, 21] and from the discussion of incidents in Section three.

Combined production and protection control systems

31 Separation of the interlocking and protection functions from the process or

machine production control functions is not always possible, but is recommended wherever reasonably practicable.

32 This separation assists safety because the resulting safety part is usually smaller and less complex, and this in turn minimises the chance of design and implementation errors. In addition, separation facilitates design features that provide security against misuse, and also design features that provide independence against failures in the production control system part.

33 However, where the risk from the machine or process is low, or where separation would actually increase complexity, eg in some machine control systems, it may not be appropriate to separate control and protection.

34 It is essential that where production and protection control systems do overlap, their design should ensure that any change made to the production control system does not reduce the safety integrity of the protection system.

Process or machine production control systems

35 The purpose of the process or machine production control system, on the other hand, is to assist operators by providing them with a continuous flow of information on plant status, alarm annunciation, and records of performance, as well as its main function of ensuring that the product is to specification. It therefore follows that it is good engineering practice to design the process or machine production control system to minimise the frequency of demands placed upon the interlocking and protection systems. If operator response to alarms is critical to safety, then a dedicated system of high safety integrity may be required. In any event, careful attention needs to be paid to human factor issues[5, 6, 7, 8, 22].

36 Appendix two gives an overview of the overall safety lifecycle approach to identifying the safety role a control system should perform. Also described in

Appendix two is the control system lifecycle, which provides a systematic approach to minimising design and implementation errors in the control system itself.

SECTION THREE: CONTROL SYSTEM FAILURES

37 This section describes a number of incidents where failure of a control system can be attributed to errors or omissions in a discrete phase of that system's lifecycle. The circumstances surrounding each incident is first described, followed by a commentary giving guidance on possible solutions.

38 A simple classification scheme has been devised for analysing the causes of the incidents included in this document (see Table 1). The scheme has been developed from the safety lifecycle as described in Appendix two.

39 This incident classification scheme allocates errors and failures to the phase where the root causes of the incident originated. For example, a failure in a control system during maintenance might be traced back to errors and mistakes made during the specification phase. Five phases have been used, and some of these have been sub-divided, giving a total of eight categories under which the incidents have been classified (see Table 1).

Phase	Description
1	**Safety requirements specification**
	● Functional requirements specification
	● Safety integrity requirements specification
2	**Design and implementation**
3	**Installation and commissioning**
4	**Operation and maintenance**
	● Action by operational workers
	● Maintenance activities
5	**Changes after commissioning**
	● Modification and retrofit
	● De-commissioning

Table 1: Incident classification scheme

40 Most incidents happen because of errors in more than one phase, and it is often difficult to judge which error is the most significant. For this publication, a judgement has been made as to which project phase was predominant, and the description of the incident recorded under that phase. Others may have differing views. The results of the analysis are included in tabular form in Appendix one, where only the primary cause has been included in column totals.

Safety requirements specification

41 With reference to Table 1, this phase starts with the original idea or concept for the project. The objective is to produce a clear and precise description of the safety requirements, which can be divided into two main classes. Functional safety requirements are the safety requirements related to the intended purpose of the plant or equipment. They ensure that plant or equipment maintain a safe state (this does not include other safety requirements such as insulation designed to prevent electric shock). Safety integrity requirements are related to the 'failure-free' performance of a safety system.

42 In the early days of a project, the requirements for functional safety of a system could be called safety objectives, because the functions required of the safety systems will not be fully identified until detailed design has been completed.

43 The main activity within this phase is hazard and risk analysis of an appropriate level of formality and rigour. The requirements for functional safety are divided into two separate specifications, the first details the safety functions, and the second the level of safety integrity.

Specification of safety functions

44 Safety functions are the actions needed to prevent equipment failing and causing a risk of injury or ill-health. In engineering terms they are requirements that cause a plant or machine to move to or maintain a safe state.

45 The specification of safety functions makes explicit the requirements needed to prevent risk of injury or ill-health throughout all operational modes of the plant or equipment - setting up, normal use, cleaning and maintenance.

46 Making safety functions explicit enables proper safety assessment both in a technical way, eg by hazard and risk analysis techniques, and in a managerial way in terms of organisational procedures, eg auditing. Such techniques and procedures ensure that the overall management of health and safety in a company is adequately addressed. *Successful health and safety management*[23] gives further guidance. The specification need not be a separate document but could be a sub-section within the project's requirements specification.

47 The concepts of safety objectives and safety functions can be illustrated by the water level control of a shell-type steam boiler. One of the safety objectives for such a boiler would be that there should be 'a means to shut down the burner on low water level'.

48 The specification of safety functions would re-cast this objective into precise engineering forms concerning, eg the precision of the water level measurement, and the conditions under which the measurement is valid (range limits etc).

49 As examples of inadequate specification of safety functions, consider the following incidents.

1 Specification error causes discharge to atmosphere

In a computer-controlled batch-reactor plant, the specification for the computer program for handling plant alarms contained a fundamental error. The computer was programmed so that if a fault occurred in the plant, all controlled variables, eg cooling water flow rate, would be left as they were and an alarm would go off.

The computer had also been programmed to increase the flow of cooling water to the reflux condenser immediately after a catalyst had been added to the reactor.

When a fault arose just after the catalyst had been added, the computer failed to increase the flow of cooling water, the reactor overheated, pressure increased and caused the contents to be discharged to atmosphere when the relief valve lifted.

Please refer to *An engineer's view of human error*[24] for a more detailed description of this incident.

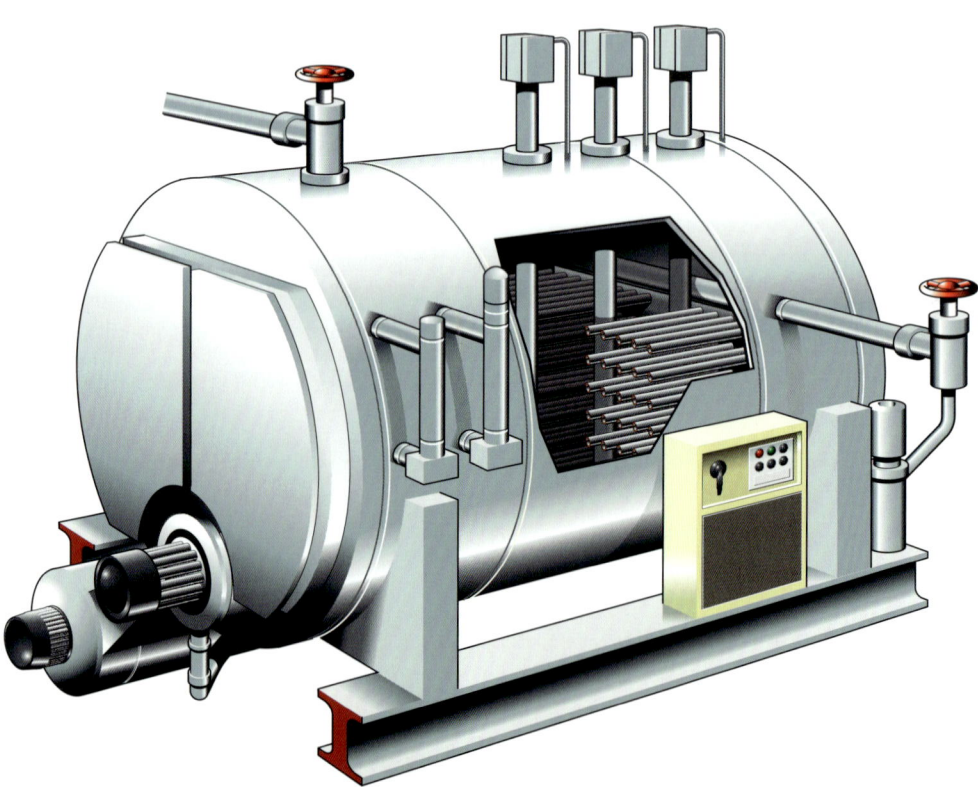

Figure 4: Shell-type steam boiler

Comment:

This incident occurred even though a hazard analysis had been carried out. Either this analysis was not thorough enough, or those carrying out the analysis made wrong assumptions about how the programmer would interpret the requirements of the design at the detailed design stage.

Whatever the reason, those concerned with both the design of the control system, and the programming of the computer, were presented with an inadequate specification of the required safety functions of the plant. The primary purpose of a specification is to provide an unambiguous way of communicating user requirements.

The effect of this particular combination of events would probably have been revealed if the specification had been analysed with respect to the particular failure modes of the control system, as opposed to adopting a general principle of 'freeze on fault'.

2 Operator traps hand in automated transit system

Part of an automated transit system included a transfer station where trays of small articles were placed onto a conveyor system by a transfer device. A jam occurred on the conveyor, and the operator of the system attempted to clear it. As he was doing so, the transfer device operated and trapped his hand.

The transfer device was controlled by a microprocessor-based system. This system included a controller with integral 'stop' button and various interfaces including one to the pneumatic control circuit of the transfer device.

Investigation when the jam was cleared found that pressing the stop button caused the transfer mechanism to move to its initial 'start-up' state, ready for production. It did not stop at its current position which is the safe course of action when a jam happens.

Pressing the stop button had caused the transfer mechanism to push against the jammed trays. Clearing the jam allowed the transfer mechanism to move, trapping the operator's hand.

Subsequent investigation found that the controller had been configured incorrectly, and that the manufacturer of the transfer mechanism, who was different from the manufacturer of the controller, had assumed that operation of the stop button would cause the controller to stop in mid-cycle while maintaining its outputs in their existing state.

Internal connections were available within the controller to enable the outputs to be maintained when the stop button was operated, but these were not used. Also, the documentation supplied by the controller manufacturer did not explain the options available for the operation of the stop button.

Comment:

Where a design is split between a number of parties, or when sub-systems are being designed concurrently, it is important that:

- there are effective communications between the relevant individuals;
- responsibilities are clearly defined; and
- a thorough review is carried out by everyone involved in the design.

This incident would have been prevented if a specification had been jointly drawn up, defining in detail the safe states of the overall system (conveyor and transfer device), and the role the stop button was to play in causing a transition to those states. At first the specification may have to be in outline

Figure 5: Operator traps hand in automated transit system

only, but eventually a detailed specification needs to be drawn up at a pre-
defined stage in the project. In this case the specification would have then
provided the baseline against which the actual design could have been
checked, and the flaw in it identified. If there is a risk of unexpected start-up
of a machine during a clearing operation, as happened in this incident, then
the requirements of the appropriate European standards[11, 25, 26] should be
applied to the machine as a whole.

Specification of Safety Integrity

50 The level of safety integrity needed for a control system flows from the hazard
and risk analysis already mentioned. Safety integrity is related to the 'failure-
free' performance of a safety system.

51 As the risk increases, either in terms of severity or probability of injury, it is
clearly more important that the safety system does not fail.

52 Failures can be classified as 'random' or 'systematic'. Random failures tend to predominate in conventional hardware components, such as relays, and are mainly due to wear and tear. Systematic failures tend to predominate in computer-based systems and are mainly due to design errors.

53 However, both types of failure mechanism are present in all control systems to varying degrees, for example a complex or novel type of hardware may be susceptible to systematic failure. The measures needed to overcome control system failures include:

- the selection of high reliability components;
- the development of a fault tolerant architecture for the entire system, from sensors through to actuators; and
- a fault avoidance approach to the design process.

54 Further information on these points can be found in IEC 61508[10], HSC guidance[14] and other publications[16, 17]. As examples of inadequate specification of safety integrity consider the following incidents.

3 Engineer microwaves hand

A commercial microwave oven rated at 10.5kW had been installed in a factory, and modified to conform to the requirements of the existing control systems. It operated satisfactorily for some time. During maintenance, an engineer reported that he felt the sensation of warmth in his hands while they were in the oven, and this was traced to failure of the door interlock.

The oven doors were pneumatically operated and fitted with pneumatic and electrical interlocks arranged to work with a photo-electric sensor to detect oven contents; this constituted a single-channel control system. The microwave

Figure 6: Engineer microwaves hand

power was switched on by a contactor when the interlock indicated that the door was closed and that there were items in the oven.

The designers of the microwave oven control system had been given inadequate information about its intended use and had selected contactors on the basis that they would operate approximately four times per day. However it was estimated that in the year before the incident the contactors had actually operated approximately 200 times per day. Investigation showed that the interlock failure was due to one of the contacts failing in a dangerous way, ie with its contacts welded together.

The interlock system, being only a single channel design, failed to danger under these circumstances.

Comment:

In this case the requirements for safety integrity presented to the designers of the interlocking control system were woefully deficient. Not only was the selected contactor inadequate for the required duty, but so were the inspection, testing, planned maintenance and replacement procedures required to ensure its continuing safety integrity. In addition, the safety design of the single channel control system was inadequate for the safety duty placed upon it.

Given the potential severity of the hazard, and the frequency of the demands on the safety system, a single channel design did not have sufficient safety integrity. The eventual solution involved an additional diverse safety interlock channel, the upgrading of the duty frequency of the contactors and the establishment of an appropriate planned preventative maintenance regime.

4 Computer failure results in potential risk to operators

One of a number of computers controlling a chemical plant failed, resulting in the inappropriate setting of a number of process valves. Operating staff were potentially put at risk, as an opportunity existed for molten polymer to be discharged from pressurised autoclaves onto the casting floor before the normal casting operation.

Investigation revealed that an integrated circuit had failed in the microprocessor that controlled the operation of an input/output interface. The failure was such that the processor set all signals for the output devices to logic 1 (all valves to open).

The mains supply at this works suffered from high levels of transient interference which the voltage regulator of the interface power supply was not specified to handle. The voltage regulator eventually failed, which in turn caused the failure of the integrated circuit in the processor.

Failure of the microprocessor had been anticipated in the original design of the computer system, but the failure detection mechanism contained a design flaw. Fault detection was by a 'watchdog' circuit configured to trip when a status 'bit' flipped to zero - thereby indicating a physical failure of the processor.

However, when the integrated circuit failed it set all bits, including the status bit, to logic 1, the opposite to the state needed to trip the watchdog, so the failure was not recognised.

Subsequent investigation also revealed that there were over 90 defects in the software, although none played any part in this particular incident.

Comment:

The root cause of this incident was that computer control had been superimposed upon an existing plant previously controlled by traditional technology. No hazard and risk analysis had been carried out before this change, and no safety integrity requirements specification had been developed.

The company carried out a detailed investigation into this incident with a hazard and operability study (HAZOP), which included examining in detail the failure modes of the computer, and their effects on the control system as a whole.

An important finding of this HAZOP was that the computer or programmable system should be studied at the same time as the process design, not in isolation or retrospectively.

Further advice on the inclusion of computer failure modes in a HAZOP can be found in *System safety: HAZOP and Software HAZOP*[27].

Also, the costs of this study, and those of implementing its findings, were estimated to be ten times those that would have been incurred if the work had been done within the original project.

The plant was re-commissioned under computer control only after the quality of the power supplies had been improved, the defects discovered in software corrected, and the fault detection scheme improved. The watchdog circuit was now configured to recognise a sequence of bits specifically generated in each cycle to check the operation of the interface processor.

Design and implementation

55 This phase starts with the safety requirements specification (comprising both safety functions and safety integrity), and results in the machine or process ready to work but prior to installation.

56 Design can be thought of as a sequence of specifications of increasing detail which finally result in a detailed design solution to the safety requirements specification, which can then be implemented. As design proceeds there is potential for errors to be made, particularly if the design becomes complicated.

57 For the shell boiler example of paragraph 47, the specification will have defined the safety integrity requirements for the burner control system. As detailed design proceeds, a specification for the 'low water' relay will have to be made. Inadequate attention to detail here could result in, for example, the specification for the contact material of the relay being unsuitable for the required duty.

58 Design errors can be minimised by adopting a formal procedure for reviewing or verifying the design at appropriate stages in the process; such verification exercises are the main method of preventing errors within the design phase.

59 Implementation is the manufacturing or fabrication process. For a boiler this covers the manufacture of parts, their assembly into the burner control system and their functional testing, but not their adjustment before being installed and taken into use.

60 As examples of inadequate design, consider the following incidents.

5 Out of sequence cut caused by a flywheel guillotine

In a paper-cutting guillotine, the knife was mechanically driven via a crankshaft which was connected through a combined clutch-brake unit to a flywheel powered by an electric motor. A photo-electric light curtain was fitted to prevent the operation of the knife while paper was being loaded into the machine. The control system could be programmed to move the paper forward by operating the back gauge so that a number of sequential cuts could be made.

The operator set up an automatic program, and part of the way through the guillotine made a cut in the wrong place. The knife then returned to top dead centre, the back gauge moved forward again and another false cut was made. Fortunately the operator was not injured.

The control system on this machine was primarily electronic but used relays where higher current capability was needed. Various control functions were derived from the operation of position switches on cams driven from the crankshaft.

Extensive investigation found that the contacts of one of the cam-operated switches were of the wrong current rating. The use of an electronic control system, operating at low voltage and low current was not compatible with the use of a high current capacity switch. The switch depended upon a certain level of arcing during use to burn away any oxide deposited on the switch contacts. When required to switch an extremely low current of less than 1 mA, no arcing occurred, and as a consequence deposits had built up on the switch contacts. This resulted in a high electrical resistance, which the electronics interpreted as the switch contacts being open when in fact they were closed.

This is an example of an incorrectly specified switch, which failed to switch correctly because the system operating requirements regarding currents etc had not been fully considered during the design phase.

Comment:

While it is commendable that conservatively rated equipment is installed in safety-related circuits, it is necessary to determine whether they are suitable for the proposed duty. In this instance, the switched current could have been made larger, or a switch with low resistance contacts could have been supplied. It is essential that the contact material of such switches is correctly specified; gold is preferred for low current circuits operating much below 50 volts.

In general terms, it is important that attention is paid to the failure modes of every safety-related circuit during the design phase. A formal technical review of the control system during detailed design would have identified this error.

6 Runaway of travelling bridge crane

An overhead travelling bridge crane with a main hoist capacity of 450 tonnes was being controlled from a pendant control console suspended from the main cross-travel carriage. The operators went for a break, leaving the crane stationary but energised, and found on their return that the crane had moved without anyone operating it. Fortunately the crane was halted by the end stop. If it had moved in the other direction, there could have been serious consequences.

The crane used thyristor-controlled DC motors operated by a closed-loop speed control system using both electronic and magnetic amplifiers.

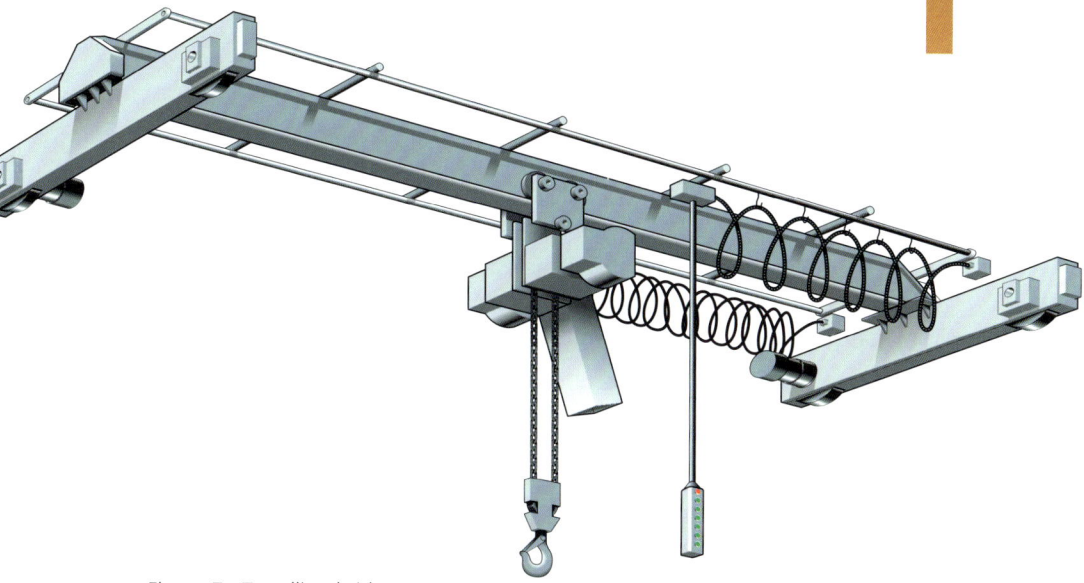

Figure 7: Travelling bridge crane

The control system and thyristor amplifiers were temperature sensitive and therefore required cooling by ventilation fans that were supplied through the main contactor.

When the crane was stopped it was left with the main contactor energised because of the requirement to keep the ventilation fans running. A failure in the electronics forming part of the speed control system generated a speed signal and, as a result, the crane moved.

Comment:

This incident shows the need to consider safety requirements for all modes of operation, including any standby modes, during the design process.

There were a number of unsatisfactory features of the design of this control system:

- it was effectively single channel, so that failure of a single component could affect safety, eg loss of feedback signal; and

- the control system could not be isolated from the power side because of the need for cooling.

The solution involved changes to the power distribution arrangements so that the control system and ventilation fans could be supplied from separate circuits. It was then possible to leave the crane unattended safely with the ventilation fans running, but with the control system de-energised.

Recommendations were also made to examine the safety integrity of the components in the control system itself to see whether improvements were needed. Such improvements could be in the form of higher reliability components or in the adoption of the fault tolerant design philosophy (see paragraphs 22 and 23 of Appendix two).

7 Mis-read VDU screen leads to acid spillage

Many tonnes of acrylic acid were lost down the drain when an operator opened the wrong valve at a chemical manufacturing plant.

A feature of the control system design enabled the operator to actuate designated items of equipment direct from a list of plant items displayed on the computer VDU.

To do this, the operator first 'called up' the relevant schedule of plant equipment, then used the keyboard to enter a two digit number denoting the equipment's position on the schedule.

In this incident, the operator inadvertently called up a schedule of equipment relating to a section of the plant on which he was not working, and consequently the wrong valve was operated.

Comment:

The displays of plant schedules were similar in format and numbering, so it is understandable that the operator was deceived into believing that the correct valve had been operated.

Where such a single failure could cause a hazard, the design needs to be such that the chance of failure is minimised, and if failure does occur, it will be detected so that recovery can be made.

In this case, the feature enabling operating commands from the keyboard could have been limited only to graphical representations of plant, therefore reducing the possibility of error.

Additionally, the software could have been designed to conduct a dialogue with the operator to verify control commands. A prompt for the operator to confirm the last instruction was a possible option, but this would only have been effective if it drew attention to the operator's mistake. In any case, it is always preferable to identify equipment by means of a unique plant number, rather than using a number relative to its position on a schedule.

This incident shows the need to consider the operator as part of the safety-related system and to adopt appropriate ergonomic and human factor principles during the design stage[5, 6, 7, 8].

Installation and commissioning

61 In this phase, finished products are configured and adjusted so that they are ready for use. Installation and commissioning can range from connecting a plug to an item of portable apparatus, to the complex task of connecting new sensors and actuators to a new control system spread over a considerable area. In the case of a shell boiler, for example, this would entail the final adjustments

being made to the burner control system before handing over the boiler for performance testing.

62 As an example of inadequate installation and commissioning, consider the following incident.

8 Chemical plant gas release

At a computer-controlled chemical plant, a reactor gas valve opened unintentionally, causing the waste gas vent line to rupture and release noxious gases to atmosphere.

Checks established that there had been no programmed or manual operation of the valve, which was subsequently found to be working correctly. The investigation therefore turned to the control system and finally to the output interface of the computer.

The output interface contained three types of interface card communicating across common addresses and data highways to the main control system. Extensive investigation of the incident traced the cause to a fault on the output driver card that caused the gas valve to operate.

The fault was identified as the omission of a ground connection (nominally zero volts), for bit number 15 on the data highway terminal which in this instance was being used as an additional address line. This meant that the card address was not unique, and it was in fact responding to commands and data from the control system that were intended for a different card altogether.

It was discovered that this fault affected two such gas valves and had been present for the six years since the control system was commissioned. Its presence was revealed only by the particular combination of plant states before the incident.

Comment:

Since the reactor gas valve was required to 'freeze' if the output driver card failed, the valve was controlled from an output card that provided a train of pulses. These cards allowed for a choice of positive or negative going pulses by providing two input connections for bit 15 on the data highway, the unused input requiring to be connected to ground potential. It was the omission of this connection that caused the pulse output card to respond to messages intended for an on/off output card.

Contributory factors include inadequate pre-delivery inspection, which overlooked the missing connection, and the questionable design decision to rely on the status of a single bit in the addressing sequence of this safety-related system.

Figure 8: Chemical plant

This incident demonstrates the importance of detailed installation and commissioning procedures so that there is no compromise of the safety integrity built into the system. Installation and commissioning procedures need to be specified as explicitly as practicable, with supporting documents that are signed by the installation technician after thorough inspections and functional tests. Monitoring of such documentation, and recording resultant changes or temporary measures, plus participation in installation and commissioning activities by technical management, will then ensure that these procedures are followed.

Operation and maintenance

63 Operation entails all those activities inherent in the normal running of the plant. Maintenance includes activities designed to check that equipment is operating to specification, and to restore equipment to that original specification if necessary. Maintenance activities may be carried out on a planned preventative basis, or as a reaction to a breakdown. This definition excludes activities intended to bring the equipment up to a new standard, which are considered in this document to be encompassed by the term modification.

64 Consider the following two examples of inadequate operation and maintenance.

9 Operator loses hand on hydraulically operated guillotine

The machine involved in this incident was a hydraulically-operated, paper-cutting guillotine, which had been fitted with a photo-electric guard to prevent it operating while paper was being loaded into the front of the machine. Under normal conditions, operation of two 'hold-to-run' push buttons - one for each hand - would result in the work material being clamped and then cut, followed by the clamp and blade then retracting. However, in this instance the clamp and blade were actuated as the operator interrupted the light curtain, amputating his hand.

Figure 9: Use of a hydraulically operated guillotine

The control system used push buttons and electrical relays to operate valves that allowed hydraulically powered pistons to move the clamp and the blade up and down. Within the control circuit there were two parallel systems used to protect against simultaneous failure; each system comprised six separate components, any one of which could stop the guillotine from working.

The machine had recently been supplied after being reconditioned, and had developed a leak from the hydraulic valve that controlled the direction of the guillotine blade. A service technician replaced the valve, but because the connecting wires of the solenoids were not marked, the technician initially connected them up incorrectly. When the machine did not operate on test, the technician returned to the rear of the machine to change over the connections of the solenoids.

It was at this point while the technician was at the rear of the machine that the operator approached from the front, and interrupted the light curtain. The guillotine operated, amputating his hand.

Investigation confirmed that the electrical connections to the 'up' and 'down' solenoids of the replacement valve had indeed been transposed. Interruption of the light curtain in these circumstances caused the blade to move downwards, instead of upwards to its safe position.

Also, no barrier or signs had been erected around the machine to warn of possible danger.

Comment:

The cause of this accident was an unfortunate combination of poor design for maintenance, and inadequate maintenance procedures which allowed an operator to approach a dangerous area. Maintenance activities need to be carried out under the supervision of a competent person, and implemented through a safe system of work. The work needs to be thoroughly planned before starting, carried out by staff who have been given appropriate training, and the work area secured to prevent unauthorised entry, possibly by the use of temporary barriers.

HSE guidance on the application of photo-electric safety systems to machinery[28], requires an additional monitored dump valve to be fitted after the directional control valve. The installation of such a valve on this guillotine would have prevented this accident, as the protective system would then have no longer been vulnerable to wiring errors in the control system. Separation of the protective functions from the control functions in this way is recommended whenever practicable.

Later designs of hydraulic valves in these machines are now equipped with plugs and sockets designed to BS 6361:1988 for their electrical connections, so that transposition of connections is not possible.

This incident shows the need to consider maintenance requirements during the specification and design of equipment, therefore reducing the possibility of hazard caused by maintenance error. Designing for maintenance activities involves not only the obvious criteria of access and ergonomic layout of equipment, but also the consequences of error on the part of the maintenance technician. 'Designing in' simple features such as colour coding of components, or unequal cable lengths, would assist the maintenance technician when working under pressure.

10 Man crushed to death by food factory hoist

In a food factory a system of conveyors was used to move trays of prepared food to and from a chiller room. This room was equipped with entry and exit hoists, and the complete system was controlled by computer. It had been reported that a hoist was faulty, and it was during the investigation and repair of this item that a man was crushed to death while attempting to reconnect a proximity switch to the control system.

Information was fed into the computer using a code for the product and a further code for the destination within the plant. The computer also used the outputs of proximity switches and position encoding devices, to determine where the trays of food were within the system.

A means of power isolation for the hoist drive motor had been provided but was not used and the man was attempting to reconnect the loose wires of a proximity switch while the computer was still in an operational mode.

Two of the three wires required had been successfully reconnected, but reconnecting the final wire had the effect of sending a signal to the computer, which initiated a downward movement of the hoist, crushing the man making the connection.

Comment:

Dangerous parts of machinery should always be enclosed to prevent access. Where access is necessary, as in maintenance operations, the isolator should have been used to remove power from the actuators before maintenance staff can gain access to the equipment. A safe system of work, eg a 'permit to work' procedure, would also have been appropriate under these circumstances to ensure that the power stayed off whilst there was any possibility that staff remained inside the enclosure.

When access is required with a control system energised, as in machine setting or fault-finding, then safety must still be maintained. One solution is to design the interlock system that protects the operator in such a way that when it is placed in its 'setting' mode, it automatically engages a restricted mode of operation that cannot be overridden. Examples include 'inching' or slow motion modes of operation, and diagnostic modes in computer-controlled plant where special programs are run to diagnose faults.

In these circumstances it is vitally important that the control system that places the machine or process in its restricted mode of operation has a high safety integrity. Such a control system would shut the equipment down safely and prevent a re-start when a signal indicating an unsafe condition is detected, or when a fault or failure occurs within the control system.

In this case, because of the potential for severe injury, the equipment should have been disconnected from the supply, and a safe system of work prepared to cover the repair, testing and revalidation of the equipment against its safety specification. Isolation and the immobilisation of equipment by mechanical means are the best methods of ensuring safety during maintenance operations.

Changes after commissioning

65 This phase includes all work on a machine or plant that, while still complying with the original specification, no longer complies with the current operating requirement. It includes modification, retrofitting, and de-commissioning.

Modification and retrofit

66 This is defined as any activity where the intention is to change the specification of a machine or plant. This is distinct from maintenance, where the intention is to restore the equipment to its original specification. Changes resulting from modification and retrofit need to be controlled to ensure that safety is not impaired.

67 Often overlooked is the impact of the change on other safety-related systems. The impact of a change should therefore be assessed using hazard and risk analysis techniques, and the design specification for the modification subject to the same design review procedures as those applied originally.

De-commissioning

68 The de-commissioning of an item of plant is often seen as a low risk activity. However, where the equipment operates as part of an assembly or process, its removal may affect the safety of the remaining plant. Typical issues relevant to control systems during de-commissioning include:

- inadvertent disconnection of power to other safety-related systems;
- inadvertent disconnection of signal transmission cables;
- ensuring that the safety of affected plant is maintained by other means if

alarms and interlocks need to be overridden or suppressed during de-commissioning; and

- ensuring that proper procedures are followed to authorise, control and document all modifications, whether temporary or permanent.

69 After de-commissioning has been completed, issues requiring attention include:

- ensuring that proper procedures are followed for the safe removal of all temporary modifications;
- revision of drawings;
- revalidation and re-documentation of software;
- updating control panel/VDU graphics;
- revalidation of alarms and interlocks; and
- reappraisal of sensor and actuator location, etc.

70 The general principle to adopt is that the work arising from de-commissioning should be subject to at least the same level of management control and review as was applied to the original installation.

71 Consider the following two examples of inadequate modification and retrofit.

11 North Sea drilling rig lists

A semi-submersible drilling rig changed ownership, and the new owners wanted extensive modifications to be carried out. After modifications were completed the rig carried out various drilling tasks in the North Sea. It was then put into a storage area for six months due to a lack of work. When the vessel was put into service during the next drilling contract, it started to list following a power failure. After power was restored it was found that some of the control valves of the ballast control system were not fully closed, and that leakage past them was causing the rig to list. The crew were standing by life-boats, and the list was 16 degrees by the time the fault was found and the system brought back under control.

In normal operations, the drilling rig was kept level by pumping water between various ballast tanks, and the valves between the ballast tanks were electrically controlled and hydraulically operated.

During modifications to the rig, the ballast control valves were made fully hydraulic, ie hydraulic control and actuation. In addition, two electrically operated safety shut-off valves were installed in the main hydraulic supply line to each of the two operating consoles to protect the ballast system. In the event of electrical supply failure, these valves were expected to release the hydraulic pressure in all ballast valve operating lines, causing the ballast valves to close so the trim would 'freeze'.

Comment:

Investigation found that a crucial filter in the hydraulic system, although specified for this conversion, had not been fitted, and this had allowed pipe debris to collect in the safety shut-off valves. The seals of these valves were damaged when the valves operated during the power failure, allowing hydraulic fluid to pass into return lines when power was restored. This in turn caused back pressure to develop in the actuators of the ballast control valves, which partially opened and caused the rig to list.

The primary cause of the incident was the omission of the filter. However the investigation also showed that procedures for flushing pipe debris from the hydraulic system after modification were inadequate. Also, the design of the modified control system had not been properly validated, and was inherently unsafe.

Although the hydraulic system had been flushed out, the manner and sequence of flushing was not specified, and it is believed that debris and foreign material remained in the system. Where a complex system is being re-commissioned, it is particularly important that a specification for the work is defined and implemented. Apparently simple tasks such as fitting a filter and flushing out a pipe system can be made ineffective by inadequate attention to detail and an absence of project procedures.

The design of the hydraulic system was poor as the capacity of the return line proved to be inadequate to cope with the effect of mechanical damage to the seals of the safety shut-off valves.

Although the need for a filter was recognised, it should have been expected that debris would inevitably collect in the hydraulic system, and the capacity of the return line should have been designed to take this failure mode into account. These shortcomings would have been revealed if a formal safety validation had been carried out on the proposed modifications. The checks on the design were in fact very poor, and did not even include revised flow or pressure calculations.

Where a modification of a safety-related control system is contemplated, the safety requirements specification should be reviewed to confirm that the proposed modification will not reduce the original safety integrity of the design.

12 Radiation shield doors malfunction

A monitoring cell (essentially a special room), was used to handle highly radioactive material. It was equipped with inner and outer shield doors originally designed to operate like an air lock, ie only one door could be open at any one time. However, modifications were later made to the key exchange system controlling their operation to allow both doors to be open, but only under certain conditions during maintenance activities.

Following such a maintenance activity, an operator used the in-cell crane to lift a process container into the monitoring cell, but noticed in the background on his TV monitor that both shield doors were open, and after closing the inner door reported the failure. Fortunately no-one was in the immediate vicinity of the doors, otherwise a significant radiation dose could have been received.

The operation of the doors was safeguarded by a number of distinct systems. Firstly there was an administrative system, prescribed by procedures which involved a formal permit-to-work. Then there was the main automatic safety system, provided in the form of a key-exchange system operating in conjunction with a hard-wired interlock; this was designed to prevent the opening of the outer door if the radiation level between the doors was high. Finally there were two software-based interlocks associated with the programmable logic controller (PLC) controlling the operations in the cell.

Either of these software interlocks should have prevented a radioactive container being introduced into the cell while both doors were open. The incident happened due to the combination of weaknesses in the permit-to-work system, design faults, and inadequate modification procedures associated with the engineering of the protective systems.

The subsequent investigation into the failure revealed the following.

- Cell entry procedures and permit-to-work procedures were not extensive enough.

- Under certain conditions, the key exchange system did not hold the keys captive and, together with the modifications to the key exchange system, it permitted process operations in the cell with both doors in the open position. The fact that the keys were removable while both doors were open represented a significant design fault which persisted throughout the original commissioning and throughout any additional commissioning after the modification. Also, the hard-wired radiation monitor between the shield doors provided no protection in this incident, as it was only designed to prevent the opening of a closed door. In this case the cell outer door was already open when the radiation source was introduced.

■ A change had been introduced into the PLC interlocking software during the modification to allow both doors to be open simultaneously. This change had not been devised by the design staff and had not therefore been subjected to testing. It contained a simple coding error which rendered the interlock it would have provided ineffective.

■ Software providing an interlock between the cell inner door and the position of the in-cell crane was overriden by another software modification which had been authorised under a Temporary Plant Modification Proposal (TPMP). This TPMP was regarded as the quickest option to enable maintenance to be carried out on in-cell equipment under prevailing plant conditions, and within the timescale of available resources. Details of this software modification were recorded in the TPMP book, and by endorsement of the work permit.

Comment:

This incident happened because three separate changes had been implemented in the engineering of protective systems at different times in the lifecycle, and none had been properly controlled or validated. The following points should be noted.

■ The effect of modifications to the key exchange system had never been fully analysed, and the shortcomings in the modified system had not been recognised during commissioning.

- The software changes were regarded as having a minor influence on safety and, as they were intended to improve matters, were only required to undergo a local check, ie no formal hazard assessment had been carried out.

- The software modification required by the TPMP had been correctly recorded but then forgotten. The endorsement on the work permit was either ignored, or the proper procedure for handing back the plant to production was not carried out. In any case, the need to reverse the temporary modification to the software went unnoticed.

Subsequent action has seen the re-design of the shield doors interlocking system, together with the identification of the protective systems and their implementation in hard-wired form separate from the PLC control system. The permit-to-work procedure, and monitoring cell entry procedure, were also revised. It was recognised that both temporary and permanent modifications need to be correctly categorised for appropriate safety assessment.

The practice of carrying out appropriate hazard assessment before modifications are implemented has been reinforced. These assessments are now being reviewed by staff who are independent of operating management.

SECTION FOUR: ANALYSIS OF INCIDENTS

72 Table 3 in Appendix one lists all the incidents that were used in the analysis, and identifies the causes of each against the classification given in Table 1 on page 12. Although most incidents had only one major cause, some incidents had more than one cause, and a total of 56 causes were identified for the 34 incidents.

73 This data has been grouped in Table 2, which gives the percentage of the primary causes attributable to each lifecycle phase. Figure 10 presents these figures in a pie chart.

Primary cause by phase	Frequency	Phase%
Inadequate functional requirements specification	4	12
Inadequate safety integrity requirements specification	11	32
Total inadequate specification	**15**	**44**
Total inadequate design and implementation	**5**	**15**
Total inadequate installation and commissioning	**2**	**6**
Inadequate operation	1	3
Inadequate maintenance	4	12
Total inadequate operation and maintenance	**5**	**15**
Inadequate modification	7	20
Inadequate de-commissioning	0	0
Total inadequate change control after commissioning	**7**	**20**

(These figures are represented graphically in Figure 10)

Table 2: Classification of primary causes

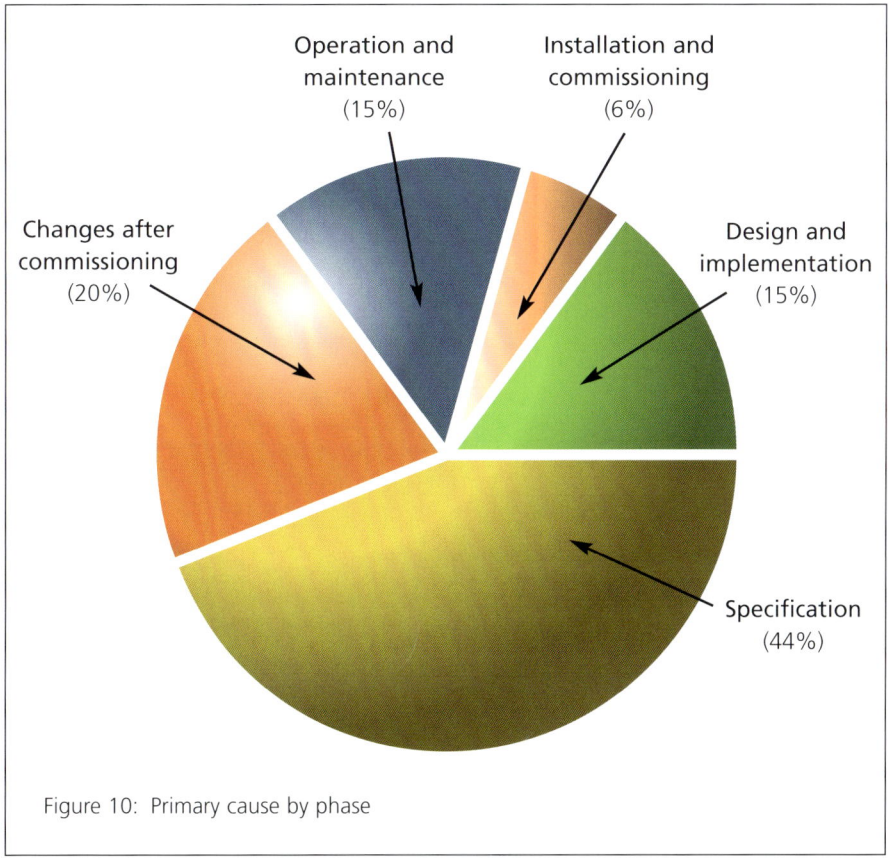

Figure 10: Primary cause by phase

Commentary

74 It is acknowledged that because of the small sample size the results of the analysis have low statistical significance, and therefore care needs to be taken in using these results to generalise for all control system failures. Even so, there are many useful lessons to be learned from summaries of incidents such as these.

75 The analysis suggests that most control system failures may have their root cause in an inadequate specification. In some cases this was because insufficient hazard analysis of the EUC had been carried out; in others it was because the impact on the specification of a critical failure mode of the control system had not been assessed. The control system needs to be continually

reviewed throughout all lifecycle phases, both from the perspective of the EUC and the detailed design and implementation of the control system itself. Otherwise the end result is a machine, or plant, with inadequate protection against the hazard.

76 Other studies provide support for these conclusions. In the area of software development a number of studies have shown that errors made during specification account for most software faults and failures[29, 30, 31].

SECTION FIVE: MANAGERIAL RESPONSIBILITIES

77 The foregoing analysis looked at incidents mainly in terms of technical measures. An alternative view would be to look at the incident causes as a means of identifying key staff within an organisation, whose action could have prevented the occurrence of such incidents.

78 This is important in the context of the Management of Health and Safety at Work Regulations 1999 (see Section one and Appendix three). It is the duty of employers to carry out an assessment of the risks to the health and safety of their employees and others (Regulation 3), and that organisational arrangements and procedures address safety as a critical topic at all phases of a system's life (Regulation 5). It is senior managers' responsibility to formulate safety policy and then to foster the development of a safety culture throughout all levels of the organisation. For further advice see *Successful health and safety management*[23].

79 Responsibility for safety at the operational level is shared between multi-disciplinary groups of people working as teams at all stages in the life of equipment, whether the equipment is a machine, a control system, or a continuous chemical process. It is therefore vital that communication between these groups is effective. Whatever form the functional organisation takes, it is management's responsibility to develop and then monitor reporting procedures to ensure that communication remains effective.

80 Operational and maintenance procedures will also need to be developed, and adherence to them continually monitored. It is management's responsibility to ensure that all such procedures are well understood, unambiguous, simple to implement and adequately documented to provide an audit trail.

81 Training and experience of workers are important factors in the prevention of accidents. People are vital to the success of any commercial organisation, and management should ensure that the workforce is adequately qualified, trained, and experienced to carry out the tasks required. This is not a 'once and for all' event, but a continual process of performance appraisal to identify training needs, and a corporate commitment to the provision of training.

82 From an economic viewpoint, managers have the task of balancing the demands of economic production with their general responsibilities under the Health and Safety at Work etc Act 1974. It has been shown that even for relatively simple organisations, the costs of accidents can be significantly greater than the costs associated with accident prevention[4].

SECTION SIX: CONCLUSIONS

83 The majority of accidents described in this publication were not caused by some subtle failure mode of the control system, but by defects that were preventable if a systematic approach had been adopted throughout its lifecycle. Failure to pay attention to detail, particularly during the specification phase of a project, and to properly manage technical issues were the root causes of these accidents.

84 Two important general conclusions can be drawn:

■ the engineering and management principles employed to ensure safety throughout the life of a control system are the same whatever the underlying technology used; and

■ although it is not possible to anticipate all causes of control system failure, most can be anticipated if a systematic risk-based approach is employed throughout the life of the system.

85 The main cause of control system failure was inadequate specification. This was due to either:

■ poor hazard analysis of the equipment under control; or

■ failure to assess whether foreseeable failure modes of the control system would compromise the specification of the system.

86 The technical causes of many incidents often cut across traditional professional disciplines, and it is important that a systematic approach is used to identify hazards. Where assessment shows that the consequences of failure

present little risk to people or the environment, or when the design is simple, then a systematic approach based on experience and checklists may be adequate to identify hazards. Where the consequences of failure present significant risk to people or the environment, or when the design is complex, then formal hazard identification techniques, eg HAZOP[27, 32], are recommended.

87 It is important to continually review the design as engineering proceeds to ensure that the specification is not compromised by the selection of the wrong components, or by weaknesses in the design itself. For simple systems, or when the consequences of failure present little risk to people or the environment, design analysis using a systematic approach based on experience and checklists may be adequate. For complex systems, or when the consequences of failure present significant risk to people or the environment, design analysis using a formal safety technique such as failure modes and effect analysis (FMEA)[33] is recommended.

88 There is a tendency to be over-optimistic about the reliability of single channel systems. The principle that 'no single failure should cause a dangerous failure of the overall system' should be seriously considered. Critical components and sub-systems will often need duplication to achieve the required level of safety integrity, but this should not be interpreted as a general exhortation to duplicate or triplicate every component.

89 A balanced view will need to be taken when considering the level of redundancy required, so that the overall complexity is commensurate with the risk, and defects due to both random and systematic faults minimised. Unnecessary over-complication of the control system due to duplication may also result in an increase in operator and maintenance-induced faults; simplicity is the key to reliable safety functions.

90 Independence and separation of safety systems from other parts of the system is strongly recommended wherever it reduces complexity. In addition, the design should aim to reveal all significant failures so that fault treatment, by manual or automatic means (as appropriate), can take place.

91 If operator interaction with the control system is important for safety (eg the need to react to an alarm), then the operator/equipment interface should be designed to take account of ergonomic principles such as information feedback and verification. The detail of control panel layout, or data layout on a VDU, may mean the difference between a correct or incorrect selection of a function, eg the closing or opening of a valve.

92 It is important that software used in safety-related control systems is produced using quality assurance[34] and software safety engineering techniques[35].

93 Maintenance operations also need to be considered at the specification and design stages. Equipment should be constructed or adapted so that:

■ maintenance operations that involve a risk to health and safety can be carried out while the equipment is shut down; or

■ maintenance operations can be carried out without exposing the person carrying them out to a risk to health and safety.

94 Further information can be found in Section 6 of the Health and Safety at Work etc Act 1974 and Regulation 22 of the *Provision and Use of Work Equipment Regulations 1998*[36].

95 Inadequate reporting of defects, poor resource allocation and training, and questionable competency of staff, were all found as contributory factors in the

incidents. When allocating work to employees, employers should ensure that the demands of the job do not exceed the employees' ability to carry out the work without risk to themselves or others. Employers should take account of the employees' capabilities and the level of their training, knowledge and experience. If additional training is needed, it should be provided. Further information can be found in Regulation 13 of the *Management of Health and Safety at Work Regulations* 1999[37] and the IEE Competency Guidelines[38].

96 Any maintenance work should therefore only be carried out by those who have received adequate information, instruction, and training relevant to that work. In addition, employers should continually review their arrangements for effective health and safety management of operational and maintenance procedures.

97 The modification of a plant or machine is never a simple task. Poor information on the safety features of the control system can compromise safety, particularly during maintenance and modification activities. Manufacturers and suppliers must provide sufficient information on the equipment under control (EUC) and the EUC control system, including drawings, to make safe maintenance and modification possible. For example, the original safety requirements specification is a useful document. Its availability would allow a thorough technical analysis to be carried out of the effect that the proposed modification would have on the safety of the system, before the modification is carried out.

98 It is important that new and modified installations are thoroughly tested before being taken into use.

99 The causes of failure in the control systems discussed are fairly typical and show, with hindsight, that most failures could have been avoided. It has been suggested to HSE that engineers, by their very nature, tend to specialise and may not therefore have the breadth of knowledge needed to identify and deal

with all the safety problems raised in this publication. One of the goals of this publication is to make engineers and their managers aware of the type and nature of failures in control systems, and broaden their safety knowledge.

100 Many of the features for designing safe control systems are those that are advocated for quality and business excellence. It is HSE's experience that companies who have a good health and safety performance are generally also commercially successful. This relationship seems to arise because such companies adopt a structured and systematic approach to all their activities - a philosophy strongly advocated in this publication.

APPENDIX ONE: SUMMARY OF CAUSES

Incident	PHASE							
	Functional requirements 1.1	Safety integrity 1.2	Design & implementation 2.0	Installation & commissioning 3.0	Operation 4.1	Maintenance 4.2	Modification 5.1	De-commissioning 5.2
1 Specification error causes discharge to atmosphere	■	●						
2 Operator traps hand in automated transit system	■							
3 Engineer microwaves hand			●			●		
4 Computer failure results in potential risk to operators	●	■						
5 Out of sequence cut caused by a flywheel guillotine			■					
6 Runaway of travelling bridge crane			■					
7 Mis-read VDU screen leads to acid spillage		●	■	●				
8 Chemical plant gas release		●	●	■				
9 Operator loses hand on hydraulically-operated guillotine			●			■		
10 Man crushed to death by food factory hoist						■		
11 North sea drilling rig lists								
12 Radiation shield doors malfunction			●	●			■	
13 Amputation at friction clutch press brake						■	■	
14 Repeat strokes by a flywheel powered guillotine		■						
15 Runaway radio controlled crane	●	■					●	
16 Interlock failure on process plant		●					■	
17 Vessel explodes in oil refinery	■		●		●	●		●
18 Lift moves during refurbishment							■	

54

	4	11	5	2	1	4	7	0
19 Boiler explosion								
20 Operator trapped by conveyor system		■				●	■	
21 Power disturbance causes chemical plant incident		■				●		
22 Unexpected movement of CNC machine kills operator		■				●		
23 Injection moulding machine amputates operator's finger						■		
24 Brick making machine injures maintenance staff							■	
25 Plant shuts down when instrument supply fails			■					
26 Domestic gas fire incident				■				
27 Computer breakdown causes emissions of toxic chemical			■					
28 CNC machine tool crashes into base plate					■			
29 X-ray over exposure		■						
30 Dam flood gates open								
31 Nitric acid damages plant	■	■				●		
32 Release of toxic chemical		■			●		■	
33 Automatic guard closes onto operator's hand		■						
34 Man trapped by computer-controlled vehicle		■						
Totals	**4**	**11**	**5**	**2**	**1**	**4**	**7**	**0**

Notes: **1.** Primary cause indicated with ■   **2.** Contributory cause indicated with ●   **3.** Totals are for primary causes only   **4.** Incidents 1 to 12 are described in Section three

Table 3 Summary of incident causes

APPENDIX TWO: SAFETY LIFECYCLE MODEL

1 **The safety lifecycle is presented in this document as a useful tool in the development of safety-related control systems. It should be stressed that it is not a legal requirement to use this approach; other ways may be used to satisfy legal obligations (see Section one and Appendix three).**

2 Section two discussed safety of control systems in general terms and related it to the concept of risk and 'reasonably practicable' precautions. It is, however, useful to distinguish between primary causes of danger such as electric shock and secondary or indirect causes such as control system failures that trigger other events that lead to danger, eg fire, release of toxic materials, repeat stroke of a machine etc. Functional safety ensures that plant or equipment maintains or moves to a safe state in the advent of a secondary or indirect cause of danger. The safety lifecycle concept has been developed to provide a tool for addressing this aspect of safety.

3 The safety lifecycle model is contained in IEC 61508[10], although the safety lifecycles shown here have some small changes to reflect the incident classification scheme of Section three.

4 Plant and equipment are regarded as having a useful life, after which they may be modified or taken out of use. It is therefore appropriate to think of this life as a cycle of interconnected stages, or phases, from conception, through specification, manufacture, installation, commissioning, operation, maintenance, modification, to eventual de-commissioning. This idea is well established in project management and in the application of quality assurance. It is also increasingly being used as a model to focus attention on the

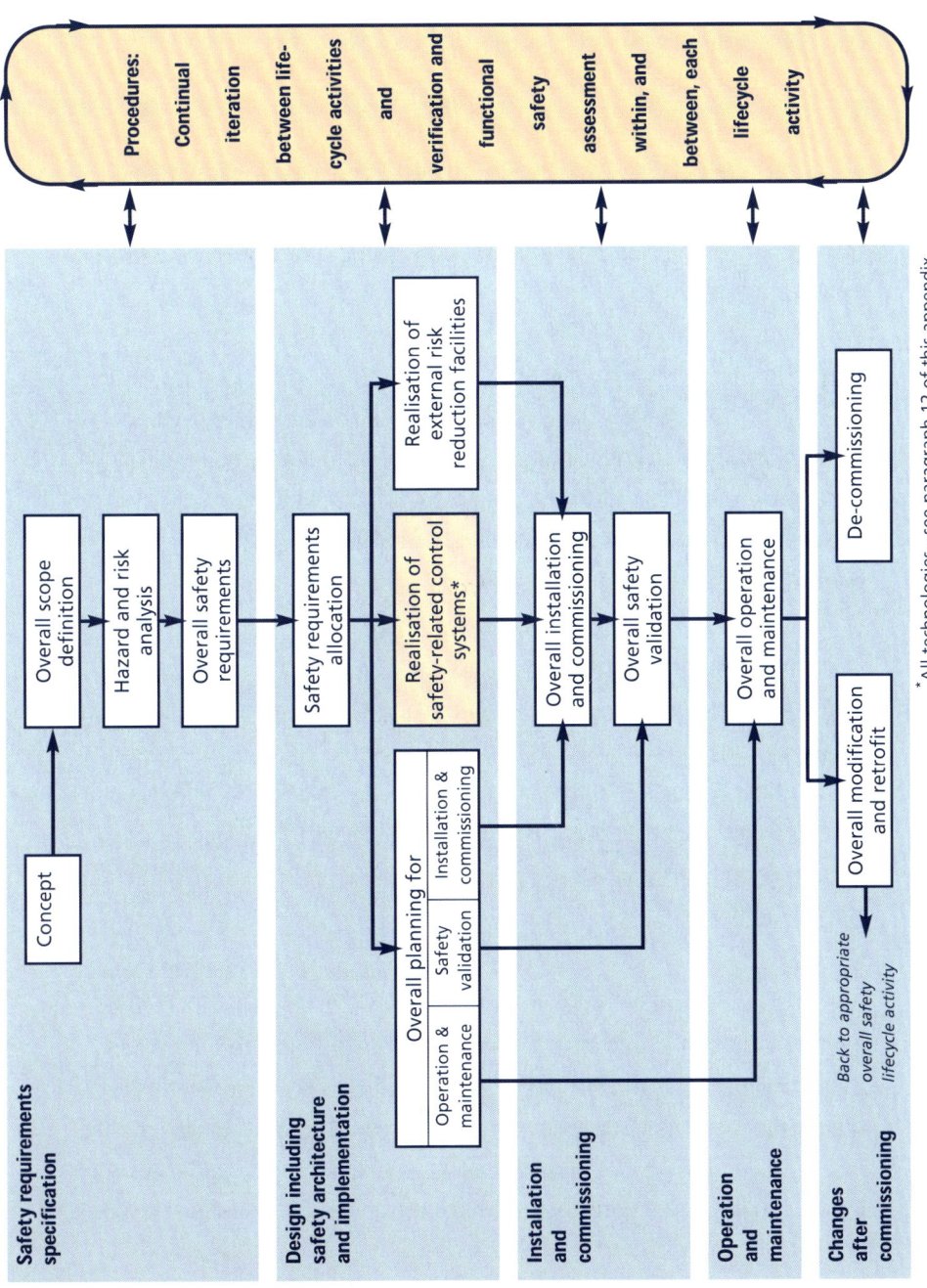

Figure 11: Overall safety lifecycle model

* All technologies - see paragraph 12 of this appendix

importance of safety as a discrete function in every one of the above stages. The safety lifecycle is defined as:

'The necessary activities involved in the implementation of safety-related systems, occurring during a period of time that starts at the concept phase of a project and finishes when all of the safety-related systems are no longer available for use.'

5   The safety lifecycle phases are shown as rectangular boxes in Figure 11 (the meaning of the larger shading is discussed later). Each phase has an input, a defined objective, a set of associated safety activities, and an output, or 'deliverable'. The deliverables of one phase provide the inputs to the next, the phase objectives being described in more detail in Table 4. Running across all the lifecycle phases are verification and assessment activities.

6   In common with the project model, the safety lifecycle model is essentially a 'top-down' approach. It is also evident that the safety lifecycle is modelled as a flowchart of interconnected activities, rather than a series of discrete blocks with functional labels. The fundamental difference between the project and safety lifecycle models, however, is not in the way the safety lifecycle is portrayed, but in its formalised use of procedures for the assessment and verification of results of each activity.

7   Many of the incidents analysed for this publication were found to be due to faults in equipment whose impact had not been considered in the overall safety requirements specification. To minimise the chance of this happening, it is necessary to formally review 'upstream' activities to establish whether their results are affected by subsequent decisions as progress is made through the safety lifecycle. These formalised procedures give the overall safety lifecycle its essentially iterative character.

ACTIVITIES	OBJECTIVES
Concept	To develop a level of understanding of the equipment under control (EUC) and its environment (physical, legislative etc) sufficient to enable the other safety lifecycle activities to be satisfactorily carried out.
Scope definition	To determine the boundary of the EUC and the EUC control system. To specify the scope of the hazard and risk analysis (eg process hazards, environmental hazards etc).
Hazard and risk analysis	To determine the hazards and hazardous events of the EUC and the EUC control system (in all modes of operation), for all reasonably foreseeable circumstances including fault conditions and misuse. To determine the event sequences leading to the hazardous events. To determine the EUC risks associated with the hazardous events.
Overall safety requirements	To develop the specification for the overall safety requirements, in terms of the safety functions requirements and safety integrity requirements, for all safety related systems and external risk reduction facilities, in order to achieve the required functional safety.
Safety requirements allocation	To allocate the safety functions, contained in the specification for the overall safety requirements specification (both the safety functions requirements and the safety integrity requirements), to the designated safety-related systems and external risk reduction facilities. To allocate a safety integrity level to each safety function.
Overall operation and maintenance planning	To develop a plan for operating and maintaining the safety-related systems, to ensure that the required functional safety is maintained during operation and maintenance.
Overall safety validation planning	To develop a plan to facilitate the overall safety validation of the safety-related systems.
Overall installation and commissioning planning	To develop a plan for the installation of the safety-related systems in a controlled manner, to ensure that the required functional safety is achieved. To develop a plan for the commissioning of the safety-related systems in a controlled manner, to ensure that the required functional safety is achieved.
Realisation of safety related control systems	To create safety-related control systems conforming to the specification for the safety requirements (comprising the specification for the safety functions requirements and the specification for the safety integrity requirements).
Realisation of external risk reduction facilities	To create external risk reduction facilities to meet the safety functions requirements and safety integrity requirements specified for such facilities.
Overall installation and commissioning	To install the safety-related systems. To commission the safety-related systems.
Overall safety validation	To validate that the safety-related systems meet the specification for the overall safety requirements, taking into account the safety requirements allocation.
Overall operation and maintenance	To operate and maintain the safety-related systems in order that the required functional safety is maintained.
Overall modification and retrofit	To ensure that the functional safety for the safety-related systems is appropriate, both during and after the modification and retrofit phase has taken place.
Decommissioning	To ensure that the functional safety for the safety-related systems is appropriate in the circumstances during and after the activities of decommissioning the EUC.

Table 4: The overall safety lifecycle

8   To avoid unnecessary repetition in the diagram, the safety lifecycle of Figure 11 shows hazard and risk analysis once only, but in reality this activity can only be of a preliminary nature at this point in the lifecycle. Hazard and risk analysis is used continually throughout the safety lifecycle, and particularly during the 'realisation' activities shown within the design and implementation boundary.

9   It is stressed that because this model is designed to be as general as possible it is necessarily very detailed. Simple projects where the hazards and risks are well understood may not need to use all the phases or carry out all the safety activities within each phase; therefore it is expected that tailoring to the problem in hand will be required. Formal hazard and risk studies are recommended where a system is so complex that the ways in which it can fail are not immediately obvious. Examples include fault tree analysis[39], failure mode and effect analysis[33] and hazard and operability studies[27, 32].

10   The safety lifecycle does not require a particular organisational structure. Many project phase 'boundaries' can be superimposed to suit administrative procedures and organisational requirements. As an example, a particular project structure has been superimposed on the safety lifecycle in Figure 11, in the form of the larger shading. Many other project structures will be possible.

11   It is also stressed that the safety lifecycle does not require the completion of one activity before starting another; a 'concurrent design' approach can be used.

12   In conclusion the advantages of the safety lifecycle model are:

■   it provides a clear view of the entire problem;

- it provides a reference point for all parties involved in the project, and minimises the risk of an 'isolationist' culture within each phase (particularly if subcontractors are involved), which can be a potential impediment to the achievement of the overall safety objective;

- it supports the risk management approach required in legislation;

- it supports the technical requirements of the legislation on safety of control systems (see Section one and Appendix three); and

- it enables the need for documentation to be properly identified, and ensures that such documentation is appropriate to the needs of preceding and succeeding phase activities.

The control system safety lifecycle

13 The following sections describe an application of the safety lifecycle model for control systems that have a safety role - the control system safety lifecycle - which has the same philosophy and iterative characteristics as the overall model. This is shown in Figure 12 and includes an expansion of the realisation phase of the overall safety lifecycle model of Figure 11. When applied to the engineering of control systems, the control system safety lifecycle is relevant to all safety-related control systems irrespective of the technology employed.

14 Safety-related systems are designed to prevent the EUC from going into a dangerous state by taking appropriate action on receipt of commands. The failure of a safety-related system would be included in the events leading to the identified hazard or hazards. Although there may be other systems having safety functions, it is the safety-related systems that have been designated to achieve, in their own right, the required level of safety.

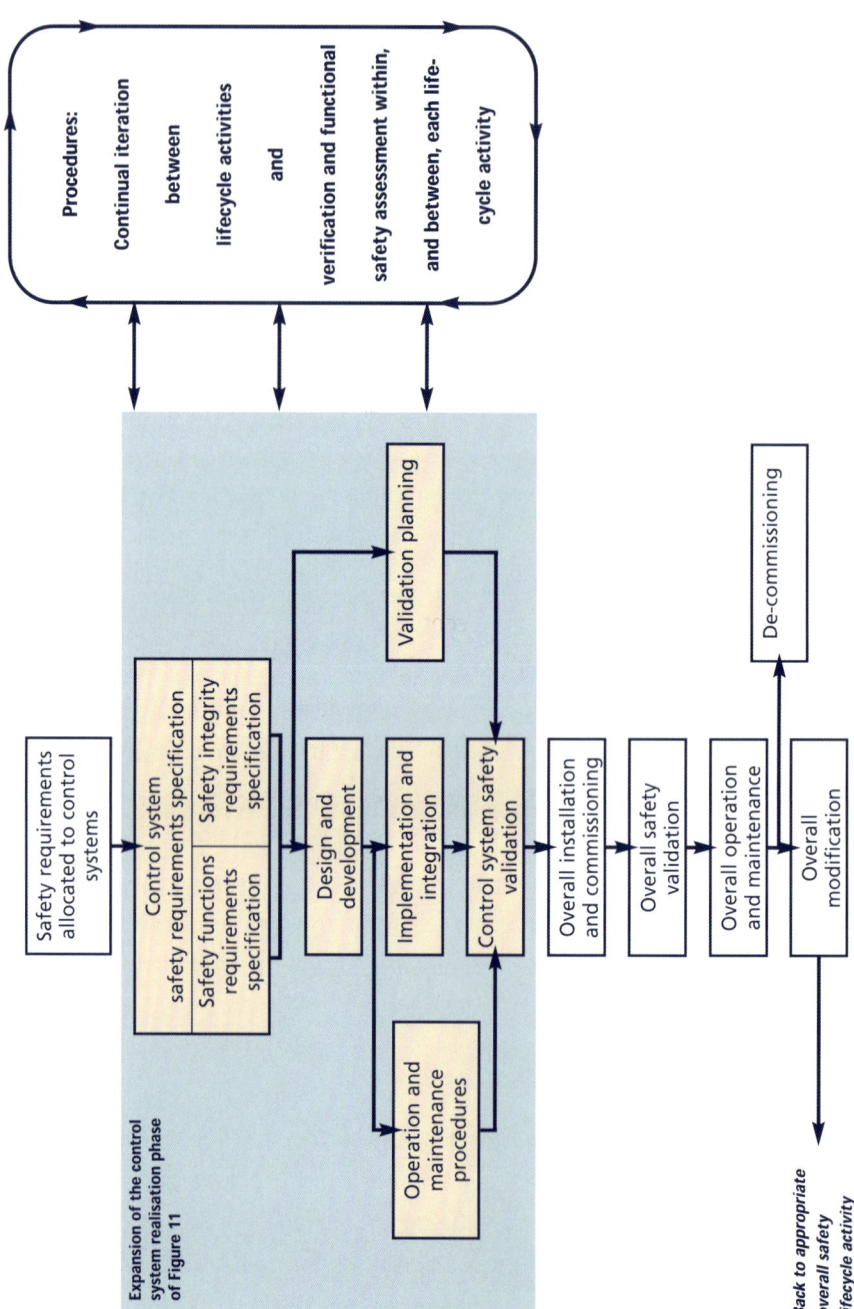

Figure 12: Control system safety lifecycle

Requirements specification for safety-related control systems

15 The safety-related control system specification is made up of two elements:

- the safety functions requirements of the system - what functions have to be achieved; and

- the safety integrity requirements - how reliable the safety functions should be.

16 The safety functions requirements are an expansion of the requirements allocated to the control system in the design and implementation phase of the overall safety lifecycle. Examples of these requirements are interlocking functions and protection functions, as described in paragraphs 27 to 30 of Section two.

17 The required safety integrity of the control system is defined by the results of the hazard and risk analysis carried out on the equipment under control (EUC). Consideration of the severity of the hazard, and the anticipated frequency of occurrence, will then dictate the level of safety integrity required to reduce the degree of risk associated with the EUC to an acceptable level.

18 The safety integrity level can be expressed quantitatively, eg as a probability of failure on demand for safety-related protection systems, or qualitatively, eg by specifying that the system should be capable of carrying out its safety function in the presence of a specified number and type of fault for a specified period of time.

19 The more detailed the specification for the safety-related control system, the less interpretation will be required of the designer, with consequent reduction in the chance of an error being made. Certainly design staff should never be expected to work in isolation from those who write the specification; close liaison between these two groups is essential if errors in interpretation are to be avoided.

Design and development

20 Two key techniques employed in designing for safety are fault avoidance and fault tolerance. Fault avoidance techniques are used by the designer to address the problems posed by the complexity of the system, and by the susceptibility of the system to 'built-in' (systematic) modes of failure. The more complex the design, the more prone the system will be to systematic faults with consequent increased effort to ensure that faults are discovered and removed. This is a major issue in the development of software, for example.

21 Fault avoidance strives to make the chance of occurrence of a particular failure mode sufficiently low so that it becomes commensurate with the risk. Selection of high reliability or high quality components is one example of this method.

22 When using fault tolerance techniques on the other hand, the designer accepts that faults will occur, but that the system will tolerate them for a specified period. The control system could be designed so that faults will be revealed, and dealt with safely by ensuring that the plant or equipment is placed in a safe state. Techniques such as redundancy, diversity, majority voting etc are used to provide fault tolerance.

23 Often, particularly where there is uncertainty that all faults have been identified, a combination of fault avoidance and fault tolerance is used in the design. Whatever the combination, the design should enable the operator to use the machine or process safely throughout all its operating cycles. Similarly, the control system should be designed to enable the safe completion of maintenance tasks for both machines and processes.

Validation planning

24 In the context of control systems, validation is concerned with demonstrating that the system meets its safety requirements specification. Experience has

shown that planning for validation should start during the design phase. It is at this point that the designer will be in the strongest position to identify the tests (or analysis methods) that would demonstrate that the needs of the user have been met. It is inadvisable to leave validation planning to a 'test engineer' devising test cases after manufacture, because the original design staff may not be available for consultation.

25 The plan should contain items such as the test environment, test procedures and pass/fail criteria. The plan should apply to all operational modes of the EUC, ie start-up, normal production, cycle/process 'hold', shut-down, maintenance etc, and also allow for reasonably foreseeable abnormal conditions.

Operation and maintenance procedures

26 The procedures for operating the control system need to be prepared well in advance of installation and commissioning. These should cover all modes of operation - automatic operation, manual operation, cleaning, cycle/process 'hold' etc - the same modes of operation as those used for planning the safety validation. Operating procedures also need to cover matters such as the method to safely clear a fault and reset afterwards, the frequency and method for the proof-testing of safety functions, etc.

27 Maintenance procedures, too, will need to be prepared well in advance of use, and need to be considered as the design evolves. In particular, it is important that the designer strives to minimise the need to bypass or override safety systems during maintenance. If this proves unavoidable, maintenance procedures should set out clearly how an equivalent level of safety is to be achieved, eg by the use of temporary barriers and a permit-to-work system. The procedures should set out how to carry out fault recording and analysis and how to ensure that the results are reviewed by the appropriate level of management.

Safety validation

28 Control system safety validation incorporates factory acceptance testing of the control systems, and comes before overall safety validation (the two distinct phases are shown in Figure 12). However, under certain circumstances, eg when hardware and application software have been supplied by different subcontractors, it may not be practicable for the safety validation of the control system to be completed before the overall safety validation.

29 In such cases, it will be necessary to complete the safety validation of the control system during the overall safety validation activity, after all hardware and software have been installed.

30 Whatever the situation, it is vital that the safety functions and safety integrity of the control system are tested in accordance with the safety validation plan, and a log of results should be kept. This log will form the basis of the validation report and should include details of the diagnostic equipment used, calibration data, and test results (including discrepancies).

Verification

31 Since the safety lifecycle is a series of interconnected activities, the output (result) of one activity becomes the input (objective) of the next. Checking that the outputs satisfy the inputs before moving on to the next safety lifecycle phase is a useful aid in identifying mistakes and errors early on in the design phase. This checking procedure is called verification.

32 The degree of rigour with which verification is applied will vary with the target safety integrity level, and the degree of complexity of the control system. For example, a simple relay design will require less checking than a complex software design where it will not usually be possible to rely on final acceptance testing to find design faults.

Functional safety assessment

33 This is a technical evaluation, carried out by personnel who are independent of the project team, to come to a decision, based on evidence, as to whether functional safety has been achieved.

34 Further amplification of the safety lifecycle is given in Section three in relation to the incidents, their causes, and solutions. Further advice on safety-related systems can be found in IEC 61508[10], guidance from the Hazards Forum[15], and other publications[20, 21].

APPENDIX THREE: THE LEGAL FRAMEWORK

1   This appendix describes the main legal requirements that have a bearing on control system safety.

Health and Safety at Work etc Act 1974

2   This Act places duties on those who control work activities to safeguard the health and safety of anyone who may be thereby affected. In particular, specific responsibilities are placed upon:

- employers to provide and maintain plant and systems of work that are, so far as is reasonably practicable, safe and without risks to health;

- the self-employed to conduct their work to ensure, so far as is reasonably practicable, that he and other people who may be affected thereby are not exposed to risks to their health and safety;

- designers, manufacturers, importers or suppliers to:

  - ensure, so far as is reasonably practicable, that articles are designed and constructed so that they are safe and without risks to health;

  - take the necessary steps to ensure that users are provided with adequate information to ensure safe use of those articles; and to

  - carry out such testing and examination as may be necessary to ensure compliance with these duties.

3   This Act also places duties on employees while at work to:

- take reasonable care for the health and safety of themselves and others who may be affected by their acts or omissions;

- co-operate, so far as is necessary, with their employer and others who have any duty imposed on them by relevant statutory provision.

The Supply of Machinery (Safety) Regulations 1992 (as amended in 1994)

4   These Regulations place duties on suppliers of machinery and set essential health and safety requirements for machinery safety. For the purpose of these regulations, 'machinery' is defined as:

(a) *an assembly of linked parts or components, at least one of which moves including, without prejudice to the generality of the foregoing, the appropriate actuators, control and power circuits, joined together for a specific application, in particular for the processing, treatment, moving or packaging of a material;*

(b) *an assembly of machines, that is to say, an assembly of items of machinery as referred to in paragraph (a) above which, in order to achieve the same end, are arranged and controlled so that they function as an integral whole notwithstanding that the items of machinery may themselves be relevant machinery and accordingly severally required to comply with these regulations;*

(c) *interchangeable equipment modifying the function of a machine which is supplied for the purpose of being assembled with an item of machinery as referred to in paragraph (a) above or with a series of different items of machinery or with a tractor by the operator himself save for any such equipment which is a spare part or tool.*

5   Section 1.2 of the essential health and safety requirements listed in Schedule 3 to the regulations is of particular relevance to control systems. It covers the following issues:

- safety and reliability of control systems;
- control devices;
- starting;
- stopping devices including normal stopping and emergency stop;
- mode selection;
- failure of the power supply;
- failure of the control circuit; and
- user-friendly software.

6   Note also that the second amendment to the Machinery Directive (93/44/EEC) has brought safety components, as defined, within the scope of the regulations. Refer to the DTI guidance notes[40].

7   An integral feature of this product safety legislation is the voluntary use of harmonised standards developed by European standardisation bodies, ie the European committee for standardisation (CEN), the European committee for electrotechnical standardisation (CENELEC) and the European telecommunications standards institute (ETSI). One way in which suppliers can show they comply with the requirements of the Supply of Machinery (Safety) Regulations is to conform to all relevant harmonised standards. Conformity with harmonised standards is not compulsory; other equally effective means are acceptable, providing they meet the legal requirement.

The Management of Health and Safety at Work Regulations 1999

7   These Regulations place a variety of duties on employers relevant to the management of control systems, among which are the following.

8   Regulation 3 requires employers to carry out an assessment of the risks to the health of their employees and the public stemming from their work activities. The purpose of the assessment is to identify the measures the employer needs to take to comply with other relevant legislation, eg the Health and Safety at Work etc Act 1974, or the Provision and Use of Work Equipment Regulations 1998. Following this assessment, employers are required to organise their activities so that the measures identified are put into effect.

9   Most incidents involving control systems have been due to inadequately specifying the purpose of the system in the first place. A thorough risk assessment as required by these regulations should help identify hazards and subsequent risks. The appropriate measures can then be identified for incorporation into the initial specification of the system.

10 Regulation 5 requires employers to have arrangements in place for the planning, organisation, control, monitoring and review of preventive and protective measures. These arrangements should be integrated with the general management system, and are required to be recorded in undertakings having five or more employees.

11 The safety integrity built into control systems can be degraded by poor operating and maintenance procedures. The adoption of a systematic approach to the planning, control and monitoring of operational and maintenance activities ensures that the design requirements are not compromised during the working life of the system.

12 Regulation 7 requires employers to have access to competent help in applying the provisions of health and safety law, unless they are competent to undertake the required measures without assistance.

13 Employers may appoint one or more of their own employees to do all that is necessary, or may enlist support from outside their organisation, or do both. Large employers may well appoint a whole department with specific health and safety responsibilities, including specialists in safety engineering, for example.

14 Regulation 13 requires that employers should ensure that the demands of the job do not exceed the employees' capability to carry out the work without risk to themselves or others. Employers should take account of the employees' capabilities and the level of their training, knowledge and experience. If additional training is required, it should be provided.

15 Training needs are likely to be greatest on recruitment, and when significant changes occur in an employee's work environment. If the change includes the introduction of a completely new technology, it may bring with it new and unfamiliar risks. Competent outside advice may be needed.

16 The Management of Health and Safety at Work Regulations 1999 are accompanied by an Approved Code of Practice and Guidance[37].

The Provision and Use of Work Equipment Regulations 1998

17 The primary objective of these Regulations is to ensure the provision of safe, suitable work equipment and its safe use. They place duties on users of work equipment that mirror those placed on suppliers by the Supply of Machinery (Safety) Regulations 1992.

18 'Work equipment' means:

'any machinery, appliance, apparatus, tool or installation for use at work (whether exclusively or not)'.

19 'Use' in relation to work equipment means:

'any activity involving work equipment and includes starting, stopping, programming, setting, transporting, repairing, modifying, maintaining, servicing and cleaning'.

20 These regulations ensure, when selecting and integrating machinery with particular safety characteristics into an overall system of work, the employer takes into account the particular characteristics of the workplace and the operations to be performed.

21 Other requirements of the regulations cover matters such as safeguarding dangerous parts of machinery, the supply of information, instruction and training for operators and supervisors, and maintenance activities.

22 Regulation 18 requires that a control system shall ensure:

'so far as is reasonably practicable, that any fault in or damage to any part of the control system or the loss of supply of any source of energy used by the work equipment cannot result in additional or increased risk to health or safety'.

23 Therefore, failure of any part of the control system should lead to a 'fail-safe' condition (or correctly, a 'minimised failure to danger' condition) and not impede operation of the stop or emergency stop controls. Measures taken in the design and application of the control system to mitigate against the effects of failure will therefore need to be balanced against the consequences of that failure. The greater the risk, the more resistant the system needs to be against the effects of failure.

24 Further details may be found in the Approved Code of Practice and Guidance[36].

The Health and Safety (Display Screen Equipment) Regulations 1992

25 These Regulations set requirements for the protection of employees and the self-employed who habitually use display screen equipment as a significant part of their employment. The main provisions require employers to analyse work stations, and ensure that they meet the minimum requirements laid down in the Schedule to the Regulations. For further information see the Guidance on the Regulations[9].

REFERENCES

1   *Essentials of health and safety at work* (Third edition) HSE Books 1999
    ISBN 0 7176 0716 X

2   *Guidelines on risk issues* Engineering Council 1993
    ISBN 0 9516611 7 5

3   *Reducing risks, protecting people: HSE's decision-making process* Report
    HSE Books 2001 ISBN 0 7176 2151 0

4   *The costs of accidents at work* HSG96 (Second edition) HSE Books 1997
    ISBN 0 7176 1343 7 Summarised in the free HSE leaflet *Reduce risks-cut costs*.
    See also www.hse.gov.uk/costs

5   *Understanding ergonomics at work: Reduce accidents and ill health and
    increase productivity by fitting the task to the worker* Leaflet INDG90(rev2)
    HSE Books 2003 (single copy free or priced packs of 15 ISBN 0 7176 2599 0)

6   *Reducing error and influencing behaviour* HSG48 (Second edition) HSE Books
    1999 ISBN 0 7176 2452 8

7   M Carey *Proposed framework for addressing human factors in IEC 61508* HSE
    Contract Research Report 373/2001- available at
    www.hse.gov.uk/research/crr_pdf/2001/crr01373.pdf

8   F Redmill, J Rajan *Human factors in safety-critical systems* Butterworth
    Heinemann 1997 ISBN 0 7506 2715 8

9   *Work with display screen equipment. Health and Safety (Display Screen Equipment) Regulations 1992 as amended by the Health and Safety (Miscellaneous Amendments) Regulations 2002. Guidance on Regulations L26* (Second edition) HSE Books 2003 ISBN 0 7176 2582 6

10 IEC 61508, *Functional safety of electrical/electronic/programmable electronic safety-related systems* International Electrotechnical Commission www.iec.ch/61508

11 BS EN 60204-1:1998 *Safety of machinery - Electrical equipment of machines - Part 1: General requirements* British Standards Institution

12 BS EN 954-1:1997 *Safety of machinery - Safety related parts of control systems - Part 1: General principles for design* British Standards Institution

13 *Computer control: A question of safety* Leaflet INDG243 HSE Books 1997 (single copy free or priced packs of 15 ISBN 0 7176 1327 5)

14 *The use of computers in safety-critical applications: Final report of the study group on the safety of operational computer systems* Report HSE Books 1998 ISBN 0 7176 1620 7

15 *Safety-related systems: Guidance for Engineers* The Hazards Forum 2002 ISBN 0 9525103 0 8

16 N Storey *Safety-critical computer systems* Addison-Wesley 1996 ISBN 0 201 42787 7

17 N G Leveson *Safeware: System safety and computers* Addison-Wesley 1995 ISBN 0 201 11972 2

18 BS EN 1088:1996 *Safety of machinery - Interlocking devices associated with guards - Principles for design and selection* British Standards Institution

19 PD 5304:2000 *Safe use of machinery* British Standards Institution

20 D J Smith *Reliability, maintainability and risk: Practical methods for engineers* (Sixth edition) Butterworth-Heinemann 2001 ISBN 0 7506 5168 7

21 W M Goble *Control systems safety evaluation and reliability* (Second edition) Instrument Society of America 1998 ISBN 1 55617 636 8

22 *Better alarm handling in the chemical and allied industries* Chemical Information Sheet CHIS6 HSE Books 2000

23 *Successful health and safety management* HSG 65 (Second edition) HSE Books 1997 ISBN 0 7176 1276 7

24 T Kletz *An engineer's view of human error* (Third Edition) IChemE 2001 ISBN 0 85295 430 1

25 BS EN 1037:1996 *Safety of machinery - Prevention of unexpected start-up* British Standards Institution

26 BS EN 418:1992 *Safety of machinery - Emergency stop equipment, functional aspects - Principles for design* British Standards Institution

27 F Redmill, M Chudleigh and J Catmur *System safety: HAZOP and Software HAZOP* John Wiley and Sons 1999 ISBN 0 471 98280 6

28 *Application of electro-sensitive protective equipment using light curtains and light beam devices to machinery* HSG 180 HSE Books 1999 ISBN 07176 1550 2

29 K Kanoun and T Sabourin *Software Dependability of a telephone switching system Digest, Fault Tolerant Computing Symposium-17*, 236-241 Pittsburgh Pa June 1987

30 *High Risk Series: Information Management and Technology* General Accounting Office GAO/HR97-9 Feb 97

31 C Chambers, P R Croll and M Bowell *A study of incidents involving programmable electronic safety-related systems. Interacting with computers* 11 1999 597-609 Elsevier

32 *HAZOP: Guide to best practice* RC120 Chemical Industries Association 2000 ISBN 0 85295 427 1

33 BS 5760-5:1991 *Reliability of systems, equipment and components - Part 5: Guide to failure modes, effects and criticality analysis (FMEA and FMECA)* British Standards Institution

34 *The TickIT Guide* Issue 5.0 2001 British Standards Institution-DISC

35 IEC 61508-3:1998, *Functional safety of electrical/electronic/programmable electronic safety-related systems - Part 3: Software requirements* International Electrotechnical Commission www.iec.ch/61508

36 *Safe use of work equipment. Provision and Use of Work Equipment Regulations 1998. Approved Code of Practice and guidance* L22 (Second edition) HSE Books 1998 ISBN 0 7176 1626 6

37 *Management of health and safety at work. Management of Health and Safety at Work Regulations 1999. Approved Code of Practice and guidance* L21 (Second edition) HSE Books 2000 ISBN 0 7176 2488 9

38 *Safety, competency and commitment: Competency guidelines for safety related systems practitioners* IEE 1999 ISBN 0 85296 787 X

39 *Fault tree handbook* U.S. Nuclear Regulatory Commission 1981 NUREG-0492 Available at www.nrc.gov/reading-rm/doc-collections/nuregs/staff/sr0492/

40 *Machinery - Guidance notes on UK regulations* DTI 1995 URN 95/650 Available at www.dti.gov.uk/strd/mps.pdf

41 *IEC Multilingual Dictionary on CD-ROM* (Fifth edition) 2002 IEC

GLOSSARY

Note: Most definitions are based on those given in the IEC Multilingual Dictionary[41] or IEC 61508[10].

Address: Character or group of characters that identifies a storage location or a device without the use of any intermediate reference.

Binary digit (bit): A member of a set of two elements commonly used to represent information.

Data: Information presented in a manner suitable for automatic processing.

Error: Discrepancy between a computed, observed or measured value or condition and the true, specified or theoretically correct value or condition.

Equipment under control (EUC): Equipment, machinery, apparatus or plant used for manufacturing, process, transportation, medical or other activities.

EUC risk: Risk arising from the EUC or its interaction with the EUC control system.

External risk reduction facility: Measure to reduce or mitigate the risks which is separate and distinct from, and does not use, the safety-related systems, eg a drain system, a fire wall and a bund around a flammable liquid storage tank.

Failure: Termination of the ability of a functional unit to perform a required function.

Fault: Abnormal condition that may cause a reduction in, or loss of, the capability of a functional unit to perform a required function.

Fault avoidance: Use of techniques and procedures which aim to avoid the introduction of faults during any phase of the safety lifecycle of the safety-related system.

Fault tolerance: Ability of a functional unit to perform a required function in the presence of faults or errors.

Feedback: Principle whereby the result of a process or activity is used to modify its further development. 'Feedback control' is synonymous with 'closed loop' control in which the control action is made to depend on the measurement of the variable being controlled.

Freeze on fault: Requirement for an actuator to maintain its position under defined fault conditions, such as power failure.

Functional safety: Part of the overall safety relating to the EUC and the EUC control system that depends on the safety-related systems and external risk reduction facilities operating correctly in response to their inputs.

Functional safety assessment: Investigation, based on evidence, to judge the functional safety achieved by one or more safety related systems or external risk reduction facilities.

Ground connection: Synonymous to 'earth connection'. A connection needed to maintain a given piece of equipment, an installation, or a system, as close as practicable to earth potential, conventionally taken as zero volts.

Hard-wired: Familiar term for 'wired program control' in which the signal processing is determined by the fixed physical interconnections among a group of devices such as relays.

Note: Hard-wired systems do not contain any software.

Harm: Physical injury or damage to the health of people either directly or indirectly as a result of damage to property or to the environment.

Hazard: Potential source of harm.

Hazardous event: Circumstance in which a person is exposed to hazard(s), which results in harm.

Hazard and operability study (HAZOP): Systematic technique for identifying the hazards associated with the design and intended operation of a process.

Hazard analysis: Formal technique for identifying hazards, eg using HAZOP, and then identifying the event sequences leading to those hazards.

Highway: A common path within an apparatus, eg a computer, over which signals from a number of channels pass.

Interface: A shared boundary between two functional units defined by functional characteristics, signal characteristics, or other characteristics as appropriate.
Note: Computers operate at low levels of voltage, typically 0 to 5 volts. They therefore require both input and output interfaces to enable them to work with the relatively high voltage levels required by plant sensors and actuators.

Output driver card: An interface circuit board specifically designed to send operating signals to an output device, such as a solenoid valve.

On/Off: A signal or device having only two stable states, either 'on' or 'off'.

Programmable electronic system: System for control, protection or monitoring based on one or more programmable electronic devices, including all elements of the system such as power supplies, sensors and other input devices, data highways and other communication paths, and actuators and other output devices.

Processor: A functional unit that interprets and executes instructions. The 'central processing unit' of a computer is usually made up of one or more processors, one or more data stores (memories), and possibly change over equipment.

Pulse: An abrupt variation of short duration of a physical quantity (usually voltage in communication terms) followed by a rapid return to the initial value.

Pulse (positive): Variation in a physical quantity above a common reference level.

Pulse (negative): Variation in a physical quantity below a common reference level.

Programmable logic controller (PLC): Device capable of controlling plant or machinery, which relies on machine/plant states for the correct execution of its program in 'real' time (as it happens).

Random failure: Failure, occurring at a random time that results from one or more of the possible degradation mechanisms in hardware.

Redundancy: Existence of means, in addition to the means that would be sufficient, for a functional unit to perform a required function or for data to represent information.

Reflux: Literally to 'flow back'. In process plant usage it refers to liquid that has been condensed from vapour and then returned to a reactor or distillation column.

Risk: Combination of the probability of occurrence of harm and the severity of that harm.

Risk analysis: A technique for evaluating risk.

Safety lifecycle: Necessary activities involved in the implementation of safety related systems, occurring during a period of time that starts at the concept phase of a project and finishes when all of the safety related systems and external risk reduction facilities are no longer available for use.

Safety related control system: System that carries out active control of the EUC and that has the potential, if not used in accordance with its design intent, to enter an unsafe state.

Safety related system: System that implements the required safety functions necessary to achieve or to maintain a safe state for the equipment under control, and is intended to achieve, on its own or with other safety-related systems or external risk reduction facilities, the necessary safety integrity for the required safety functions.

Safety requirements specification: Specification containing all the requirements of the safety functions that have to be performed by the safety related systems. This is divided into two parts:

- *Safety functions requirements specification:* specification containing the requirements for the safety functions that have to be performed by the safety related systems.

- *Safety integrity requirements specification:* specification containing the safety integrity requirements of the safety functions that have to be performed by the safety related systems.

Systematic failure: Failure related in a deterministic way to a certain cause, which can only be eliminated by a modification of the design or of the manufacturing process, operational procedures, documentation or other relevant factors.

Terminal: A component provided for the connection of a device to external conductors.

Validation: Confirmation by examination and provision of objective evidence that the particular requirements for a specific intended use are fulfilled.
Note 1: In the context of safety, validation is the activity of demonstrating that the safety related system under consideration, before or after installation, meets in all respects its safety requirements specification.
Note 2: Some definitions of validation in the context of safety systems include consideration of whether the actual safety requirements specification itself sufficiently and accurately presents the safety needs of the intending user. In this document, this aspect is considered to be part of functional safety assessment.

Verification: Confirmation by examination and provision of objective evidence that the requirements have been fulfilled. Examples include document reviews, design reviews, and performance tests.

Printed and published by the Health and Safety Executive

C50   12/03